PLEASURES AND PAINS

Opium and the Orient in
Nineteenth-Century British Culture

Victorian Literature and Culture Series

Karen Chase, Jerome J. McGann, *and* Herbert Tucker, *General Editors*

PLEASURES AND PAINS

Opium and the Orient in Nineteenth-Century British Culture

———❧———

Barry Milligan

UNIVERSITY PRESS OF VIRGINIA
Charlottesville and London

THE UNIVERSITY PRESS OF VIRGINIA
Copyright © 1995 by the Rector and Visitors
of the University of Virginia

First published 1995

Library of Congress Cataloging-in-Publication Data

Milligan, Barry.
   Pleasures and pains : opium and the Orient in nineteenth-century
British culture / Barry Milligan.
      p.   cm. — (Victorian literature and culture series)
   Includes bibliographical references and index.
   ISBN 0–8139–1571–6
   1. English literature—19th century—History and criticism.
2. Narcotic addicts' writings—History and criticism.   3. Opium
habit—Great Britain—History—19th century.   4. Great Britain—
Civilization—Oriental influences.   5. Great Britain—
Civilization—19th century.   6. Authors, English—19th century—
Drug use.   7. English literature—Oriental influences.   8. Opium
habit in literature.   9. Exoticism in literature.   10. Orient—In
literature.   I. Title.   II. Series.
PR468.06M55   1995
820.9'9208—dc20
                                                                94–24140
                                                                CIP

Printed in the United States of America

TO JOAN

Contents

Illustrations

Acknowledgments

As is always the case, many individuals and organizations helped to realize this book. I am immensely grateful to Eve Kosofsky Sedgwick, Robert F. Gleckner, Regina Schwartz, Thomas Pfau, and James R. Kincaid, not only for their attentive guidance through every stage of this particular endeavor but also for their ongoing comprehensive advice, encouragement, and support on all sorts of other matters intellectual, institutional, and personal. Joe McLaughlin, Naomi Wood, and Scott McEathron helped to insure that arguments were tighter and prose was sharper by generously reading and commenting extensively on numerous drafts, and they provided the motivation and support that only the best of friends can give. Similarly, Scott Harshbarger, Mark Amos, David Barrow, Charlie Paine, and Rick Bogel often took time away from their own work to discuss mine, and their intellectual vitality, generosity, and friendship made work seem like play. Julie Tetel graciously agreed at very short notice to read an early version of the manuscript; it would have been much easier for her to refuse, but by selflessly taking the harder road, she helped me out of a tight spot and earned my eternal gratitude. Several interpretations were fleshed out with the help of an outstanding group of students in two "Narcotics and Narrative" seminars I taught at Duke University in 1991 and 1992, and I am grateful to all of them for many interesting and challenging discussions. Donna Hall added to her innumerable other generous acts of friendship by taking time out of a busy schedule to photograph, develop, and print illustrations of opium smokers. A Ball Brothers Foundation Visiting Fellowship enabled me to consult the London Collection at the Lilly Library of Indiana University, research that contributed significantly to chapters 5 and 6, and I would like to thank William R. Cagle, Sue Presnell, Casey Smith, and the rest of the staff of the Lilly Library for generously sharing their knowledge and skills. Earlier versions of material that appears in chapters 5 and 6 were previously published in *Beyond the Pleasure Dome: Writing and Addiction from the Romantics* ([Sheffield,

England: Sheffield Academic Press, 1994], 93–100) and *Victorian Literature and Culture* 20 (1992): 161–77, and I would like to thank the editors of those publications. Chapter 4 was written while I was supported by a Mellon Postdoctoral Fellowship at Cornell University, and thanks are due to the staff and the other fellows of the Society for the Humanities at Cornell and to my stimulating and supportive neighbors in the English Department. Cathie Brettschneider of the University Press of Virginia believed in this project when it was little more than two rough chapters and a prospectus, and her unflagging warmth and enthusiasm, as well as her shrewd and generous advice, were vital factors in seeing it through to completion, let alone publication. Even if I should be fortunate enough to have delivered the manuscript she hoped for, that will fall short of repaying the debt I owe her. I would also like to thank Carlotta Shearson and Pamela MacFarland Holway for seeing the manuscript through copyediting with good humor and consummate professionalism. Their efforts made this a more readable book than it otherwise would have been.

Last but far from least, I am glad of this opportunity to express my constant gratitude to my family, whose boundless support made this and all other endeavors possible, and especially to Joan and Ellen, who in addition to all of that make them worthwhile.

PLEASURES AND PAINS
Opium and the Orient in
Nineteenth-Century British Culture

Of all the carnal delights that over which opium rules as the presiding genius is most shrouded in mystery. It is invested with a weird and fantastic interest (for which its Oriental origin is doubtless in some degree accountable), and there hovers about it a vague fascination, such as is felt towards ghostly legend and the lore of fairy land. There exists a strange yearning to make more intimate acquaintance with the miraculous drug concerning which there is so much whispering, and at the same time a superstitious dread of approaching it, such as, when it comes to the pinch, possesses the rustic believer in the efficacy of repeating a prayer backwards as a means of raising the devil.

Anonymous, "East London Opium Smokers"

Introduction

FOR THE PAST two centuries in a number of Western cultures, the pairing of various consciousness-altering substances and Oriental ambience has pervaded discourses about "drugs."[1] The association began with opium, but it has extended well beyond opiates and has bridged quite a span from its historically (and, for Americans, geographically) distant origins; we owe the initial association largely to Coleridge and De Quincey's treatments of opium written in England at the beginning of the nineteenth century. And it seems that temporal and spatial distance have only strengthened rather than dissipated the association; as one American critic has said, "The De Quincey tradition being what it is, many of us will doubtless dream an Oriental dream if we but look at a grain of opium."[2]

But why is the opium/Orient tradition so mutual and so powerful, and how did it get that way? Why did Coleridge and De Quincey associate opium and the Orient in the first place, and what common cultural background lay behind the associations they seem to have shared? What was it about their "visions" that so captured the interest of their contemporaries and informed the imaginations of future generations who did not necessarily even know their names? Is there some set of communal assumptions, interests, desires, that makes the pairing of opium and the Orient compelling for the broad range of historical, cultural, and political contexts in which it has flourished? I hope in this study not so much to answer these questions one by one as to suggest that their answers are numerous and intertwined. The association of opium with fantastic Oriental visions, for instance, is not easily explicable in terms of a single phenomenon—supposed chemical reactions of opium in the brain that breed the same imagery in all users, for example—but is instead both stimulus and response to a set of interrelated historical, psychological, and cultural factors. Any attempt to answer the above questions, then, must take into account a number of linked issues: (1) the British cultural consciousness of "the Orient" in the nineteenth century; (2) military, imperial, economic, and other encounters with the Orient that informed cultural products of the era (poetry, fiction, journalism, autobiography, propaganda, travel narratives), as well as general and individual attitudes toward those encounters; and (3) attitudes toward opium, its properties, and the circumstances of its use. This examination, then, will necessarily take what might be called a cultural studies approach, intersecting several disciplines, such as history, psychology, and sociology as well as literary criticism.

Insofar as any of these disciplines will dominate in these pages, however, it is literary criticism that will probably be most often recognizable in the foreground. The relationship between opium and nineteenth-century British literature already has something of a history in literary criticism. The first sustained examination, M. H. Abrams's *The Milk of Paradise* (1934), attempted to create a catalog of opium-inspired images by tracing correspondences between the writings of a number of known users of opium (Coleridge, De Quincey, George Crabbe, Francis Thompson) and to establish that the imagery these writers have in common stems directly from the opium they all used rather than, for instance, literary conventions and other cultural common ground. This assumption was challenged by the next milestone, Elisabeth Schneider's *Coleridge, Opium and Kubla Khan* (1953), which used both textual and medical evidence to argue that "Kubla Khan" was not inspired by opium as Coleridge claimed but rather owes its imagery to a complicated amalgam of influences, both cultural and psychological. Alethea Hayter's *Opium and the Romantic Imagination* (1968) returned to a position closer to that of Abrams by focusing on the question "Does opium affect the creative processes of writers who use it?"[3] Like Abrams, Hayter searches for explanations of the traits shared by putatively opium-inspired writings more within the chemistry of the drug than in its cultural milieu. Hayter's book is also representative of another critical trend that has tended to divert attention from the cultural dynamics of opium in nineteenth-century England: her discussion frequently concerns itself with moralizations about drug use.[4] A similar judgmental impulse is evident in Molly Lefebure's *Samuel Taylor Coleridge: A Bondage of Opium* (1974). Unlike Hayter, Lefebure sees opium as having destroyed rather than enhanced Coleridge's creativity, but she nonetheless falls back upon stereotypical value judgments about opiate addicts in her discussion of the process.[5] Although Lefebure is more willing than Hayter to see relations between a nineteenth-century literary culture of opium and late twentieth-century opiate users, she is nonetheless content to let already established, morally slanted categories (for example, "junkie") dictate the terms of comparison.

The first sustained treatment of opium as a complex socio-cultural force rather than primarily as an influence on the literary imagination is *Opium and the People* (1981) by social historian Virginia Berridge and addiction researcher Griffith Edwards. *Opium and the People* is indispensable as a source of historical information about opium in nineteenth-century England and suggests a number of provocative interpretations and explanations of surrounding cultural dynamics. Although it touches on some of the cultural products that deal with opium and the Orient (Coleridge, De Quincey, *Edwin Drood,* and *Dorian Gray* are all mentioned), *Opium and the People* is first and foremost a work of social history. It raises issues and charts courses for discussions of the cultural milieu of opium use in nineteenth-century England, but it also calls attention to the need for more detailed analyses of the cultural products themselves.[6]

A discussion of opium and the Orient in nineteenth-century English culture is also necessarily a discussion of the dynamics of empire, for opium was deeply implicated in British colonial activities in the East. There has been a wealth of writing about questions of imperialism over the past two decades, both in terms of its relation to cultural productions and in more general historical and sociological terms. Several critics have asserted that various discourses of the nineteenth century are complicit in a universal, if often unconscious, conspiracy of exploitation and domination, a unilateral overwriting of other cultures by a hegemonic British scribe. Patrick Brantlinger, for instance, speaks of "the one-sidedness of imperialism's discourse with 'difference,' with its other or others—its deafness to alternative voices," and he asserts that "in most British writing about Empire, English discourse and authority are imposed on imperialized peoples, often to the extent of denying them imaginary voices (and what voices are occasionally granted support imperialism)."[7] I wish to diverge from this increasingly accepted view and argue instead that, despite the undeniable momentum of appropriation in British representations of colonized peoples, the very act of attempting to speak over those alternative voices—or speak for them—induces and/or evidences a merging with those voices, exposing split, fragmented personalities and precipitating a crisis of identity in which difference is no longer locatable.[8] This blurring of identity is one important way in which the fact of the colonized subject's existence and the possibility of his or her agency have a resistive effect in the male-, white-, and English-dominated discourses I will examine, and ultimately serves to confuse hierarchies of difference and the directionality of imperial power dynamics.

Of course it is still problematic, even dangerous, to celebrate this corrosive effect as power exercised by the colonized person, for the representation is itself often an attempt on the part of the representor to dictate the parameters of the colonized party's identity, to tame her and limit her to terms that are not only manageable but also satisfy needs of the representor. And the many criticisms of such representations are hardly immune to the same kinds of moves, be they conscious or unconscious. Spivak warns against the "dangerous . . . first-world intellectual masquerading as the absent nonrepresenter who lets the repressed speak for themselves," and her caution is appropriate with respect to the work of cultural critics who declare their supposedly liberative program only to enact less obvious versions of the assimilative, exploitive moves they critique.[9] What I attempt to do in this study, however, is neither to speak for the voices spoken over by discourses of imperialism nor even to uncover them but rather to explore the corrosive effects the very possibility of those voices had upon the dominant discourses that may or may not ultimately be said to have overwritten them.

Although elaborations of the idea that there was a comprehensive Western program to dominate the East have had the important corrective effect of helping to debunk the simplistic myth that the British Empire was primarily a benevolent civilizing mission, they are nonetheless susceptible to the reductive totalizations of conspiracy theory. For instance, a statement such as the following ultimately raises more questions than it answers about individual sites and conceptions of imperialism, the Orient, and national identity: "If it could be suggested that Eastern peoples were slothful, preoccupied with sex, violent, and incapable of self-government, then the imperialist would feel himself justified in stepping in and ruling. Political domination and economic exploitation needed the cosmetic cant of *mission civilisatrice* to seem fully commendatory."[10] Such a scenario requires not only a counterintuitively unified, unchanging agent, the imperialist, who characterizes, exploits, and dominates, but also an unspecified and difficult-to-imagine subject or group of subjects to whom this imperialist's actions do or do not "seem fully commendatory." Although it would be difficult to disagree that characterizations of Eastern peoples as slothful, violent, and so on, did at least partly arise from and reinforce many of the power dynamics of empire, it is nonetheless also difficult to envision the supposedly coherent collective parties to such a direct and intentional cause-and-effect relationship. And this particular example is not atypical; it is a seemingly similar impulse, for instance, that prompts Edward Said to speak of an allegedly homogeneous "European identity" and "European culture" and to charge that "every European, in what he could say about the Orient, was . . . a racist, an imperialist, and almost totally ethnocentric."[11]

As others have also noted, this kind of totalizing conception of Europe "sometimes appears to mimic the essentializing discourse it attacks" and risks lapsing into an "Occidentalism" that merely mirrors Said's "Orientalism."[12] Furthermore, such totalizations belie the diversity of perceptions of "the Orient" throughout the nineteenth-century French and British culture Said and others critique. As Lisa Lowe observes, "The binary opposition of Occident and Orient is . . . a misleading perception which serves to suppress the specific heterogeneities, inconstancies, and slippages of each individual notion. This heterogeneity is borne out most simply in the different meanings of 'the Orient' over time"—and, one might add, over place, culture, and so on.[13] This is certainly as true of Britain in the nineteenth century as of any other cultural/historical/geographical sampling.[14] But one needs to be cautious about even such familiar formulations as "Britain" and "the nineteenth century," for those constructs themselves rival "the Orient" for heterogeneity and internal contradictions.

The methods and objectives of this study can be simply stated: what I have attempted here is a series of local, detailed examinations of nineteenth-century English cultural products that figure perceptions of and responses to opium and the East, perceptions that repeatedly negotiate a tension between attraction and repulsion, arousal and fear, or, as De Quincey characterized the poles of his response to opium, "pleasures" and "pains." I will be examining in particular the ways in which perceptions of and responses to the Orient—including fear, desire, guilt, titillation—are paralleled, mediated, and represented metaphorically by attitudes toward opium, and the ways in which these intertwined phenomena complicate notions of identity, both national and individual. It would contradict my perception of these dynamics, then, to speak of *the* imperialist project, *the* Western mindset, and so on. It has also been my aim at least to begin to sketch out some historically conditioned patterns of cultural manifestations of anxieties about the charged nexus of drugs and foreign invasion, patterns that persist not only in modern Britain but also in the current United States, where they have been omnipresent in the media and have in recent history played a prominent role in both domestic and foreign policy. Although many of the patterns I will discuss in relation to nineteenth-century Britain had contemporary parallels and counterparts in the United States—such as American involvement in the opium trade in China and resistance to it at home, and the fear and persecution of Chinese opium smokers in San Francisco in the latter half of the century[15]—the genealogy of the American patterns nonetheless also converges on Coleridge and De Quincey, who served both implicitly and explicitly as paradigms for American cultural productions dealing with opium and other narcotics during the nineteenth century. Perhaps the most obvious American mediator of their influence is Edgar Allan Poe, whose phantasmagoric tales often loudly echo the exotic opium reveries of the British authors he so admired.[16] But the influence of Coleridge and De Quincey was certainly not limited to matters of literary convention. H. Wayne Morgan discusses the "many [American] drug users" who indulged in "experimentation," and he avers that "the great early nineteenth-century models for this behavior were the English writers who first discussed opium, especially Thomas De Quincey and Samuel Taylor Coleridge."[17] David Courtwright notes that De Quincey was so established in American culture as a model of the opium habitué that American users throughout the nineteenth century were labeled as "opium eaters" after his coinage, or in a curious paraphrase as "morphine eaters," wherein the cultural persistence of the paradigm wins out over the contradictory fact that morphine was injected rather than ingested orally.[18]

The Oriental associations that surrounded opium on both sides of the Atlantic in the nineteenth century have persisted well into the twentieth. Opium smoking, for instance, has been so insistently associated with the Orient that even the 1920s Detroit opium-smoking party described by jazz musician Mezz Mezzrow is peopled with "borscht-guzzling Oriental potentates" and "looked like a scene straight out of the Arabian Nights, with the thieves and princes disguised in pinchback sports jackets."[19] William S. Burroughs paints a similar quasi-Oriental subculture of "junk" just after World War II in Manhattan, where the apartment of the first "junky" he meets sports "a china Buddha with a votive candle in front of it" and "look[s] like a chop suey joint." The face of Burroughs's junky is "smooth and brown. The cheekbones [are] high and he [looks] Oriental," and groups of such junkies swarm around a heroin dealer "like a crowd of Asiatic beggars." Their epitome is "a type of character you see only on the fringes of a junk neighborhood," whose figurative "place of origin is the Near East, probably Egypt."[20]

These Oriental associations have become so entrenched in American, English, and European cultures that they have attached themselves to other controlled substances with no discernible Oriental origins, such as the so-called psychedelics, mescaline (derived from peyote, an integral element in religious rituals of a number of native North American cultures) and LSD (synthesized from ergot, a rye fungus, in a pharmaceutical laboratory in Switzerland in 1943).[21] The chemist who first synthesized LSD described the discrepant Oriental dress of his colleagues gathered to experiment with the substance at a castle in Switzerland in 1962: "Ernest Jünger wore a long, broad, dark blue striped kaftan-like garment that he had brought from Egypt; Heribert Konzert was resplendent in a brightly embroidered mandarin gown."[22] In another controlled experiment with LSD, Anaïs Nin saw "the most delicate Persian designs," and "murals which . . . were Oriental, fragile, and complete, but then . . . became actual Oriental cities, with pagodas, temples, rich Chinese gold and red altars, and Balinese music."[23] What was a cultural and historical link in the case of opium and Oriental imagery is not easily explainable in such terms when the same imagery is affiliated with psychedelics, which seem to inherit the imagery by way of a diffuse cultural consciousness of "drugs" that is not finely discriminative. The Polish writer and graphic artist Stanislaw Ignacy Witkiewicz, writing under the influence of peyote in 1928, even professed that the direction of the inheritance was the reverse of what it might seem: "The Chinese knew peyote," he said; "all Chinese dragons and all of India come from that source," and his peyote visions duly contained conventionally Oriental images such as a pharaoh and "Egyptian and Assyrian processions."[24] Fears of foreign invasion have often been imported side-by-side with Oriental imagery, but they have also functioned independently of Oriental associations, as in the rhetoric justifying the U.S. invasion of Panama in 1989, rhetoric that often insistently linked the United States' military disruption of Panamanian cocaine trading with a defense of democracy.[25] And beginning in the late 1980s the U.S. Border Patrol at the Mexican border was supplemented by military troops assigned to exclude drug traffickers, a situation that suggests the degree to which the so-called war on drugs was perceived as a fight to fend off foreign invasion.[26]

These many parallels suggest that nineteenth-century British cultural patterns involving opium and the Orient can serve at least as a kind of test case, if not quite a genealogy, for a number of attitudes toward drugs today and during the intervening period in both Britain and the United States. A closer examination of nineteenth-century patterns can thus contribute to an understanding of the origins of contemporary attitudes—origins that are never clear-cut, even when they may appear to be. Such an understanding can be of more than a specialized scholarly value, for, as David F. Musto has said, "the absence of knowledge concerning our earlier and formative encounters with drugs unnecessarily impedes the already difficult task of establishing a workable and sustainable drug policy."[27] The repetitive patterns suggest that knowledge of our earlier and formative encounters is not so much absent as unconscious, and, to borrow somewhat simplistically from psychoanalytic paradigms, to make that unconscious knowledge conscious would create an opportunity to confront it, to reassess its value.

I must acknowledge, however, that I have only scratched the surface of the body of cultural products that played a crucial role in the formation of these patterns that are still with us. I have barely touched the realms of the graphic and plastic arts (such as the many drawings of Chinese opium smokers that appeared in newspapers, magazines, and books), and in addition to concentrating on written representations, I have further narrowed my focus to what Eve Kosofsky Sedgwick calls (in a similar mea culpa) the "book-writing classes." I concur with her that there is necessarily a "violence done to a historical argument by embodying it in a series of readings of works of literature,"[28] but my excuse for proceeding with my eyes open to do such violence anyway is that I believe there is an equal and perhaps greater violence inherent in putting forward an argument that attempts to be more comprehensive than it is realistically able to be. The more localized argument has a better chance of providing a textured understanding of its topic, an understanding that might then serve as a point of triangulation in the process of perceiving or drawing the bigger picture. My reasoning behind concentrating chiefly on the "canonical" productions of the book-writing classes is twofold: first, the writings of Coleridge, De Quincey, Dickens, Wilde, and Conan Doyle were widely read and powerful cultural forces (they all appeared, at one time or another, in the popular press). In other words, they were also canonical in their own time—that is, they were doing important and powerful cultural work—and an interpretation of their production and reception thus promises to provide valuable insight into the culture of which they were partly constitutive. I do, however, consider a number of "noncanonical" pieces as well, such as the periodical articles about opium dens that receive extended attention in chapter 5. The reasoning behind their inclusion is the same: they were popular, influential, and representative. The second reason for concentrating on the book-writing classes is perhaps more obvious and has been acknowledged by others before me: it is that the nonwriting classes, while representing a greater proportion of the population during the period in question here, necessarily have a more diffused, more mediated, and less easily recoverable voice to be examined.[29] I would be disingenuous if I did not also acknowledge a third, institutional reason for such a concentration: my academic training comes primarily from departments of English literature.

Of the additional acts of violence I knowingly commit, some are glaring (I am sure) and others are more subtle (I hope). Many readers will notice that, having already limited the range of my argument to the book-writing classes, I seem to have further limited it exclusively to the men of that class. This, however, is not so much a matter of personal preference as it is an interesting feature of nineteenth-century British writing about opium and the Orient: all of it seems to have been produced by white men. Although women did write about opium, the nexus of opium and the Orient that otherwise so often dominated the discourse about the drug seems to have been absent from their work. In *Middlemarch,* for instance, George Eliot portrays the surgeon-apothecary Lydgate's use of opium in treating a case of delirium tremens (a widely embraced use of the drug by the medical professions at the time) and details his own progressive dependence on the drug for emotional escape. Her narrator also tells us that, in a frustrated bid to follow the examples of Coleridge and De Quincey, Will Ladislaw "had made himself ill with doses of opium" trying to "evolve the genius [that] had not yet come."[30] But she never foregrounds the drug's Oriental associations. Similarly, Anne Brontë tracks the degeneration of the laudanum-tippling Lord Lowborough in *The Tenant of Wildfell Hall,* and the novel as a whole thematizes what amounts to an anticipation of later models of addiction.[31] But Brontë, like Eliot, never casts her treatment of the drug in an Oriental light. The reasons for this gender exclusivity are undoubtedly complex—perhaps too much so to be treated adequately in this study, in which they are not analyzed at any length—but are probably due in part to phenomena similar to those that might account for the apparent restrictiveness of the male-dominated genre of imperialist adventure fiction treated by Brantlinger. As he suggests, however, "Imperialism influenced not only the tradition of the adventure tale but the tradition of 'serious' domestic realism as well," and "These apparently antithetical genres do not have separate histories, but influence and shade into each other in countless ways from the Renaissance onward."[32] The same is surely true of cultural productions that treat the intersection of opium and the Orient and those that treat only one or the other.

Perhaps the most glaring inconsistency in my argument is that, having upbraided totalizing uses of the term "the Orient," I then resort to the label myself. While this is probably a partial reiteration of the very inconsistencies I upbraid in others, my defense is twofold. First, I fear that the contradictory scholarly impulses to generalize on one hand and to specify on the other necessitate recourse to any number of such contradictions, and to strive for a certain self-consciousness—to acknowledge the contradictions within which one is mired—is perhaps the closest one can come to being consistent. Second, the cultural formations I am treating were themselves erratic in their recognition of distinctions between the various regions and peoples often grouped together as "the Orient," and this is one of the conflicts that the present study attempts to describe and discuss. Therefore, to superimpose distinctions onto cultural products that did not necessarily discriminate in such ways to begin with would only be to perpetrate a different kind of violence. Although my recycling of the term does run the risk of leveling distinctions when they are made, I am ultimately more concerned to explore the conflicts between generalization and specificity in the discourses I treat than to provide a comprehensive catalog of instances of each.

Some of the most representative examples of this contradictory tendency toward both specificity and generality come from the pen of Samuel Taylor Coleridge. Although he read widely in the cutting-edge academic Orientalism of his age and could not help but see some cultural variances between, say, India and Egypt,[33] he nonetheless also had a significant intellectual stake in leveling and/or ignoring the differences between these cultures, for he was invested in the German Higher Criticism that approached the Bible as characteristic Oriental myth rather than sacred scripture and saw it as evidence of an originary universal monotheism in the Orient. Coleridge's interest in this unifying endeavor is reflected in his career-long plans to write the "last possible epic" ("The Fall of Jerusalem"), one that would focus on a moment in which all world religions could be seen as springing from the same source somewhere in the

East and reaching their apotheosis in Christianity.[34] Thus, while he implicitly acknowledged some differences among various cultures subsumed under the rubric of "the Orient," he also had a significant stake in believing, and in convincing others, that any such distinctions were finally trivial. This slipperiness of boundaries is merely one example of a phenomenon that informs much of Coleridge's writing of the 1790s and early 1800s, a series of conflicts and anxieties over not only the internal differentiation of the Orient but also its dubious differentiation from England and the English—especially the opium user. As I will argue in chapter 2, Coleridge laid the foundation for a conception of opium as the medium of a retributive Oriental infection-invasion that not only threatens to dissolve the national identity of its user but also clouds some basic reference points for individual identity, such as gender, parentage, and even the outlines of an individually differentiated body.

If Coleridge laid the foundation, then De Quincey built upon it, as chapter 3 illustrates. Whereas Coleridge saw opium as a possible passageway through which the Orient might enter and undermine the English body and culture, De Quincey's prose suggests that the Orient was always already there. For him, opium proves to be a kind of infernal archaeological tool that uncovers the not-so-deeply buried Oriental within the English. Opium thus becomes the axis of a conflict between two paradigms of national identity that pervaded nineteenth-century discourse: (1) the definition of the (English) self in opposition to the foreign (often Oriental) other and (2) a Romantic conception of national identity as continuous with national histories and traditions, or origins. That opium undercuts both models of identity by placing them in direct contradiction to one another suggests to De Quincey that the Orient is at once both other and origin, as it lies on the other side of "a barrier of utter abhorrence" but is also "the cradle of the human race." Thus the territorial expansionism he advocates as a means of expanding the ground of British identity might instead more than defeat itself by merely extending "the vast empires . . . into which the enormous population of Asia has always been cast."[35]

This Oriental beneath the English takes on a more threatening personality in Wilkie Collins's mystery novel *The Moonstone* (1868). Collins's England is pervaded by mysteriously powerful traces of Indian culture—seductive Indian diamonds, exotic immigrants, illuminated manuscripts, and objets d'art—that so captivate the imaginations of English men and women as to render them willess and childlike, a potential threat that is realized in three ruthless Hindu Brahmins who pursue the stolen Indian Moonstone to England and threaten several English lives in their attempts to retrieve it. The mixing of English and Indian cultures, even genetics, is focused in the character of the half-Indian surgeon's assistant Ezra Jennings, whose addiction to opium renders him familiar enough with the drug's effects to deduce that it was a dose of laudanum that caused a young Englishman to enter a trancelike state and steal the diamond only to forget the whole event when the drug wore off. Thus, while he solves the mystery, Jennings also exposes a De Quinceyan alien consciousness within the mundane English one, a foreign element whose links with opium render it a physiological-psychological parallel to the seductive and dangerous Indian admixture within English culture.

This implicit reversal of Eastern colonization becomes more explicit and richly textured in later Victorian writings, as chapters 5 and 6 detail. With the influx of Oriental immigrants in the 1860s, popular journalists and fiction writers begin to portray London's East End opium dens, with both delight and trepidation, as miniature Orients within the heart of the British Empire. Popular magazines portray Englishwomen assimilated—by both opium addiction and sexual unions with Chinese opium masters—to opium dens and Oriental identities. This assimilation of women destabilizes the totemized center of English domestic life by darkly mirroring "the angel in the house" in what should be the antithesis of the sacred English hearthside, an Oriental den of vice. Dickens's female proprietor of an opium den in *Edwin Drood* combines the dynamics of both marketplace and domestic space by being "a mother to [her customers]," while John Jasper, the Englishman-addict, extends the implied reversal of Anglo-Oriental colonization by smoking opium in his suburban home as well as in the East End den.

The opium den also serves in these narratives as a lens through which the audience is invited to view the instability of the market-driven aspects of the power dynamics of empire. Although the opium wars were intimately tied to Britain's monopoly over the opium market in the Eastern colonies, for instance, many opium den narratives reverse the scenario by featuring a Chinese opium master whose exclusive ability to prepare opium for smoking gives him a monopoly over the opium market in London. "The rarity of the luxury" insures that "even though [the opium master's] den is situate in, without exception, the most vile and villainous part of the metropolis, he is regarded as a person worth visiting by lords and dukes and even princes and kings."[36] This reversal of market control implies the reversal of political control as even the Prince of Wales makes the journey to the East End den and invites the opium master to perform his services at the palace.

Toward the turn of the century the opium den narratives of Oscar Wilde (*The Picture of Dorian Gray*) and Arthur Conan Doyle ("The Man With the Twisted Lip") focus on the opium den as a point of comparison between domestic English cultural elements and exotic Oriental ones, ultimately illustrating that what seems on the surface to be differentiable as Oriental is in fact inextricably woven into the texture of "English" culture. The inconspicuous blending of English and Oriental is a symptom of the instability of a number of English institutions, for the opium den also serves as a passageway between economic classes and blurs the boundary between criminal and sanctioned behavior. While these instabilities potentially undermine the supposed foundations of English culture—chiefly in the mythologized institution of domesticity—they also open up a domain for play, a possibility exploited by Sherlock Holmes and Dorian Gray, both of whom delight in the shabby costumes and alternative personae that they—not unlike Sir Richard Burton and other "explorers" in the Orient—assume for their visits to the East End.

I

Opium, the Orient, Imperialism, and National Identity

THE CONCERNS THAT are highlighted by nineteenth-century British cultural productions dealing with opium and the Orient—broadly classifiable as anxieties about bilateral cultural exchange—are inextricable from matters relating to British territorial expansion and the very definitions of "Britishness" in the nineteenth century. It is therefore vital at the outset of a discussion of those cultural productions to attempt to contextualize, historicize, and/or provisionally define the terms that are most prominent and problematic with respect to this nexus of issues. The central terms in this case are imperialism, the Orient, opium, and national identity.

Imperialism

Perhaps the most disputed term in this list is imperialism, which has been used to refer to multiple and sometimes contradictory phenomena (economic, psychological, social, political) in various historical periods. Some historians argue that only the tail end of the period treated in this study can properly be discussed in terms of imperialism. According to this way of thinking, "the age of classical or modern imperialism began around 1880," when "the 'scramble for Africa' supposedly got under way."[1] But while it is true that imperialism as a term initially gained currency in Britain only in the latter half of the nineteenth century as a description of Napoleon III's policies, nonetheless, "between 1830 and the 1870s . . . there was frequent discussion in the press and in Parliament about the condition of the 'British Empire,'" and "most early Victorians would have been mightily shocked by any suggestion that they took no interest in that glorious manifestation of 'the genius of the race,' the British Empire."[2] In fact the notion of a British Empire was accessible enough early in the century for Captain Charles Pasley to publish an entire book called *The Military Policy and Institutions of the British Empire* (1810).

Indeed Britons had progressively pursued interests abroad—in North America, the West Indies, Africa, and especially India—beginning at least as early as the charter of the East India Company in 1600, fighting a series of battles with the Dutch in the mid–seventeenth century over trading rights in

India and Africa and engaging the French in India during the middle of the following century in a burst of similarly motivated military conflicts. Robert Clive's victory over the Nawab of Murshidabad at Plassey in 1757 and the defeat of the French at Madras in 1759 gave the Company control over the huge provinces of Bengal and the Carnatic, and by 1760 India was virtually an English colony. This position became semiofficial with the India Act of 1784 (revised 1786), which subjected the East India Company's governmental operations to the supervision of a governor-general appointed by Parliament and answerable to a similarly appointed board of control in London. This arrangement was already tantamount to direct British rule of India, for as Prime Minister William Pitt said when introducing the bill, the board's power "would consist in directing what political objects the Company's servants were to pursue, and recalling such as did not pay obedience to such directions."[3] By 1833 the Company had ceased to trade at all and was instead exclusively a governing body complete with its own civil service and army. After the infamous Indian Mutiny of 1857—in which native soldiers serving in the Company's army, or sepoys, revolted against their commanders and killed a number of British civilians—Parliament dissolved the Company in favor of overt British rule through the secretary of state. The literal crowning touch came when Victoria accepted the title of Empress of India in 1876.

This last detail was the brainchild of Prime Minister Benjamin Disraeli, who shifted Britain's imperial activities into high gear in other Oriental territories as well as India. Disraeli protected British interests in India from a perceived Russian threat with an ill-fated military expedition into Afghanistan in 1878, and he purchased a 44 percent share of stock in the Suez Canal in 1875, solidifying British power in Egypt. His intervention in the war between Russia and the Ottoman Empire culminated in his participation in the Congress of Berlin, which granted Britain possession of Cyprus, a new base from which to guard the canal and the eastern Mediterranean.[4]

In order to see imperialism as beginning only in the 1880s, then, one must restrict application of the term to the programmatic military seizure and direct official government of one nation by another. Those who define British imperialism in this way ignore earlier activities that were only a matter of degree away from such systematic expansionism and thus risk playing right into the hands of the popular late-century idea that the British Empire simply emerged on its own as an inevitable phase in the evolution of a nation destined for global leadership, or as Sir John Seeley put it in 1882, "We seem, as it were, to have conquered and peopled half the world in a fit of absence of mind."[5] Rather than subscribe to such a dangerously narrow conception of imperialism, most scholars agree to a more encompassing definition such as the one offered by Charles Reynolds:

> *Imperialism is an idea that denotes a relationship of dominion—whether ex-*
> *plicit, in the form of a political sovereignty asserted by force over subject peoples*
> *independent of their will or consent, or implicit, as a system of constraint and*
> *control exercised over peoples and territories, independent of their political organ-*
> *ization, and directing their activities to the satisfaction of needs and interests*
> *themselves generated by the system.*[6]

Under this more inclusive rubric, many of the activities of Britain well before 1880 certainly qualify as versions of imperialism. For missionary and commercial activities as well as other cultural and technological exchanges arguably contribute to the domination of one nation by another. These processes—often falling under the rubric of "cultural imperialism"[7]—were also much in evidence in Britain's dealings with other countries throughout the nineteenth century.[8]

Closely tied to imperialism, both historically and conceptually, is colonialism. Reynolds again offers a useful definition: "Colonialism is distinct from imperialism in that it denotes the settlement of territory by peoples of a metropolitan power. A colonial relationship is thus established in which indigenous peoples coexist somewhat uneasily with newcomers, with their political rights and status unresolved or equivocal."[9] Thus, while imperialism could apply to a number of interactions that are ultimately part of a relation of domination (including religious, commercial, and technological exchanges), colonialism would be limited to the dynamics of actual territorial acquisition and settlement. In the history of Britain, colonialism is often interwoven with imperialism to such a degree that the two terms are in many cases interchangeable.

Whether one calls it imperialism, colonialism, or something else, however, power relations with distant regions were a preoccupation of various nineteenth-century British cultural productions that both reflected and structured those interactions (some critics even track the cross-influences back to the arguable beginnings of British imperialism in the late sixteenth century, citing *The Tempest* as the first literary appearance of the British Empire).[10] As Daniel Bivona says, "Imperialism is not simply the good or bad conscience of nineteenth-century Britain, but rather, in an important sense, its unconscious, lurking under the surface of a variety of discourses, conditioning the possibilities for emergence of some and precluding others."[11]

The Orient

Of the geographic regions associated with British imperialism during the nineteenth century, the ones with which this study will be particularly concerned are those commonly grouped together at the time under the rubric of "the Orient," which usually encompassed roughly all of Asia and nearby islands, what Americans now refer to as the Middle East (including Turkey), and parts of northern Africa.[12] This Orient functioned on a number of charged planes in nineteenth-century British culture, for it included not only the so-called biblical lands but also the settings of the hugely popular *Arabian Nights,* the inspiration for the fashionable decor of Oriental rugs, chinoiserie, and japan-lacquered furnishings, and was the fountainhead of exotic commodities such as teas, silks, and spices. The development of British attitudes toward the Orient during the eighteenth and nineteenth centuries was also intertwined with the growth of the institutionalized study of Eastern languages, literatures, and religions, or "Orientalism," a broad-ranging field that both bolstered and thrived upon the tendency to homogenize a number of Eastern regions and cultures under one conceptual umbrella. As Edward Said says, "a specialist in Islamic law no less than an expert in Chinese dialects is considered an Orientalist by people who call themselves Orientalists . . . we must learn to accept enormous, indiscriminate size plus an infinite capacity for subdivision as one of the chief characteristics of Orientalism."[13]

Nineteenth-century attitudes toward the Orient were both reflected and structured by the literary representations of various Eastern peoples and practices that had been a consistent part of the British and European cultural scenes for centuries.[14] From the medieval accounts of the East to the first English translations of the *Arabian Nights* in the early eighteenth century through the rash of Romantic poems on Oriental themes, the English reading public showed a ravenous appetite for representations of cunning caliphs, sensual sultans, and other exotic characters in Oriental settings thick with an atmosphere of magic and violence. Cruelty and sorcery, evil and even shape-changing Orientals were the stock-in-trade of such popular tales and poems as John Hawkesworth's *Almoran and Hamet* (1761), Frances Sheridan's *History of Nourijahad* (1767), William Beckford's *Vathek* (1786), Landor's *Gebir* (1798), and Southey's *Thalaba* (1801). Tales with less emphasis on magic and more on violence include Byron's *The Giaour* (1813), *The Corsair* (1814), and *Lara* (1814); Thomas Moore's *Lalla Rookh* (1817); and Walter Scott's novels featuring crusaders fighting ruthless Saracens. Other popular tales that emphasized neither violence nor magic, but still preyed upon the sense of the Orient as wildly alien and mystical, include Johnson's *Rasselas* (1759) and Alexander Dow's *Tales . . . of Inatulla of Delhi* (1768). Accounts of supposedly actual travels to the East were also popular from the time of the crusades onward and enjoyed something of a renaissance in the late eighteenth and early nineteenth centuries.

It is noteworthy, however, that the Orient of these tales almost never included China. Before Coleridge and De Quincey's opium-tinged narratives modified the English sense of the Orient, China was associated with a different set of cultural phenomena than those of the Oriental tales. A fantasized version of China often referred to as the Isle of Cathay undergirded eighteenth- and nineteenth-century English chinoiserie, the seemingly omnipresent, quasi-Chinese decorative motifs ranging from porcelain teapots and lacquered furniture to Chinese suites of rooms ("managareths") and pseudo-Chinese gardens complete with pagodas ("sharawaradgis"). The fantasized version of China reflected in these designs owed much to the exaggerated European travel narratives that thrived in the Middle Ages. The thirteenth-century memoirs of Marco Polo, for instance, initiated a genre of ever more fantastic descriptions of China under Kublai Khan of the Yuan dynasty, tales of serene people living among exotic beasts under a perfect government. Polo's account was at least based on actual travels even if his observations appear to have been sensationalized (they were recorded and made to conform to Franco-Italian literary paradigms by Polo's fanciful prisonmate, Rustichello). But some of the most widely read Oriental travel tales, such as *The Travels of Sir John Mandeville,* were pure fabrications. These narratives nonetheless gained vast popularity and authority with a Western audience that had never seen their settings, and with the later advent of the xenophobic Ming dynasty and the closing of China to the West, readers were even more hungry for accounts of this forbidden and distant world. They read with increased interest the fictionalized tales they were now even less able to disprove.[15]

Once this fantastic vision of China gained a cultural foothold it was hard to shake, and the persistence of Chinese isolationism made more down-to-earth accounts difficult to come by even as late as the mid–nineteenth century. Western contact was severely limited by the Chinese imperial government until after the Anglo-Chinese opium wars (1839–42, 1856–60), and the small number of traders and diplomats who were grudgingly allowed to enter China at all rarely made it beyond the outlying port of Canton. At the time Coleridge claimed to have experienced the fantastic opium vision of China that inspired "Kubla Khan," Anglo-Chinese relations were severely strained due to an incident involving the Chinese government's placement of its "Celestial Empire" above all earthly ones. The English Macartney embassy of 1795 had been infuriated by Chinese demands for its participation in a masque that cast the Chinese emperor as the "Son of Heaven," "Lord of the World," and made Western emissaries pay tribute to him by crawling on their bellies as if they were "Outer Barbarians come from the darkness to worship the light."[16] Macartney predictably refused. It was uncomfortable at least for the proud nascent British Empire to be commanded to recognize another empire as superior, even if they were not yet explicitly rivals.

It is partly because of a growing sense of rivalry and mutual threat between England and China that Coleridge and De Quincey's opium-dream versions of

China resemble the violent, mysterious, and demonic Orient of the Oriental tales at least as much as they resemble the serene and beautiful Cathay of chinoiserie. Together the two writers significantly altered the traditional English conceptions of China and the Orient: they merged the demonic and the serene and inverted their mutual status as escapist settings for titillating fantasies. Unlike the escapism of the Oriental tales, the Orient of these opium visions and the ones that follow is not a comfortably external context but is instead a threateningly internal one. No longer is the Orient even arguably figured as "the malleable theatrical space in which can be played out the egocentric fantasies of Romanticism."[17] In the world of the opium vision, British consciousness is the theater and the Orient is the terrifying actor of the fantasies dramatized there.

Opium

Opium itself carried strong associations with the Orient in British culture by the beginning of the nineteenth century, partly as a result of the fantastic Oriental traveler's tales of the previous centuries. Tales such as those recounted in *Purchas his Pilgrimage* (1614), Chardin's *Travels through Persia* (1764), and Baron de Tott's *Memoires du Baron de Tott, sur les Turcs et les Tartares* (1784, translated early in the nineteenth century) all featured exotic Orientals either eating or smoking opium. The association was also augmented by the fact that the chief sources of the opium in British domestic use were all Oriental. Although there were some experiments with domestic poppy cultivation as part of the agricultural "improvement" movement from the 1790s to the 1830s, and small numbers of poppies were indigenous to the Fen counties where they had long been used in folk remedies such as "poppy-head tea," by far the majority of opium for British consumption came from the Orient. The largest share came from Turkey (80–90 percent for most of the century) with some from Persia (1.4–18.9 percent from the 1870s to the end of the century) and Egypt (0.1–15.4 percent between 1831 and 1864). Despite the East India Company's monopoly over the huge poppy crops of Bengal throughout the century, Indian imports rarely supplied more than 12 percent of the opium in British domestic use, and usually accounted for less than 3 percent.[18]

Although it provided almost none of the domestic supply of opium, the British-controlled Indian opium industry nonetheless reinforced the cultural association of opium and the Orient—especially the Company's forbidden trade with China, which accounted for the majority of British opium profits. During the first part of the century, the East India Company worked in clandestine cooperation with several smaller British commercial firms to circumvent the highly restrictive Chinese foreign trade regulations and smuggle Indian opium into China. The smuggling operations were motivated by the potential to balance the Company's deficit of trade in tea and silks with China, feed its chief source of revenue in Bengal, and realize a significant profit for the cooperating smaller firms. The outraged Chinese government responded in 1839 by confiscating and destroying all opium from British warehouses in Canton. The British government in turn launched a military campaign to "open" China to free trade with the West in the first of the so-called opium wars (1839–42), which resulted in British control of Chinese customs and the ceding of Hong Kong Island to Britain in the Treaty of Nanking (1842). A second opium war (1856–60) forced further Chinese territorial and trade concessions including the extremely reluctant legalization of opium in China with the Treaty of Tientsin (1858) and the Peking Convention (1860).

The surrounding decades in England saw a rising tide of concern about the "immoral" Indo-Chinese opium traffic, including the future prime minister Gladstone's condemnation of the "pernicious article" in the House of Commons in 1840.[19] But active resistance to the trade was narrowly based before the rise of anti-opium leagues such as the Quaker-founded Society for the Suppression of the Opium Trade (SSOT) in the 1870s. In addition to its attempts to educate the public into opposing the opium trade, the SSOT lobbied Parliament to abolish the government monopoly over Indian opium cultivation (which they wanted to see limited to the production of opium exclusively for medical use) and to withdraw British pressure on the Chinese government to accept Indian opium. Even at its height the anti-opium movement was based mostly in the elite, influential, middle-class centers of opinion at which its propagandistic journal *The Friend of China* was aimed, and it never enjoyed measurable working-class support.[20] But despite the demographic biases of the SSOT's membership, *The Friend of China* and similar publications nonetheless seem to have reached a sizable middle-class audience and to have done much to shape popular perceptions of Britain's relationships with opium and the Orient.

The increased incidence of opium smoking in China after the opium wars provided fodder for the anti-opium press and fueled the controversy in England. Additional debates arose over whether British importation of Indian opium had actually fostered opium smoking in China or merely drawn attention to an indigenous custom, and whether eating or smoking the drug was more harmful. When the anti-opium front piled on additional arguments about the alleged ill effects of opium on the Indian population, the crown finally responded decisively by launching a royal commission to inquire into the production and consumption of opium in India and to ascertain whether prohibitions were warranted. The commission's controversial report (1895) ultimately justified the status quo of the opium trade and prompted accusations that the commission's inquiries had been inordinately influenced by the Anglo-Indian government.

Whether or not the commission's dealings were aboveboard, however, the report dealt a staggering blow to the anti-opium movement, which virtually stagnated for ten years before gaining some momentum again in the early twentieth century.

Moralistic perceptions of drug use like those propagated by the nineteenth-century anti-opium movements have become such an ingrained part of the rhetoric surrounding twentieth-century drug policies in both the United States and the United Kingdom that it sometimes proves difficult for modern readers to see them as arising from specific historical conditions. But in fact opium was a widespread and unremarkable part of daily existence in Britain for well over a century before the advent of disease theories of drug use in the latter half of the nineteenth century. Opium was the active ingredient in various folk remedies made from seed capsules of the poppy, or "poppy heads," and opium-based remedies were also widely available commercially throughout the century. Before the Pharmacy Act of 1868 restricted the right to sell opium and other scheduled "poisons" to licensed pharmacists and chemists, wholesale opium was available to any retailer who cared to buy and resell it, including not only chemists and druggists but also grocers, bakers, tailors, publicans, and street vendors, all of whom sold it in various forms. Britons could buy opium in pills, powders, and plasters, liniments, lozenges, and laudanum, syrups, suppositories, and seed capsules straight off the poppy stalk. And it was relatively cheap—in fact it was cheaper than liquor, a circumstance to which many detractors attributed its widespread, supposedly recreational use among the working classes of the Lancashire industrial centers and the Fens in the '30s and '40s. Various so-called patent medicines containing opium were a medical staple of British homes almost regardless of class and included such familiar brands as Godfrey's Cordial, Collis Browne's Chlorodyne, Mrs. Winslow's Soothing Syrup for infants, and the Kendal Black Drop favored by Coleridge and Byron.[21] These medicines were used to treat a long list of common afflictions both major and minor including ague, bronchitis, cancer, cholera, diabetes, diarrhea, delirium tremens, depression, fatigue, gangrene, gout, insanity, intestinal obstruction, malaria, menstrual symptoms, neuralgia, pneumonia, sciatica, sleeplessness, tetanus, tuberculosis, and ulcers.[22]

One of the indirect results of the ready availability of opium was that the phenomena later associated with "addiction" or "dependence" went largely unremarked for the first part of the century. This was also due in part to the fact that the symptoms of dependence make their most pronounced appearance only during withdrawal from opium, a discomfort for which there was little occasion when the drug was so easy to get and readily administered by mouth. When withdrawal symptoms did appear between doses, the user often interpreted them as an independent sickness for which opium was ostensibly an appropriate treatment, and the cycle was thus invisibly reinforced without being recognized. Self-medication with opium was itself frequently a means of avoiding the expense and inconvenience of professional medical care, so medical professionals did not have consistent opportunities to observe the processes of dependence in motion. Consequently the withdrawal syndrome was much less readily observable in the early part of the century than it was later with the rise of the hypodermic injection of morphine, which was always supervised by a medical professional and with which the symptoms of withdrawal are more pronounced.

But it is a bit premature to use "addiction" and "dependence" so glibly without first discussing their history. In modern parlance, the terms are virtually interchangeable and usually refer to a range of physiological, psychological, and social effects associated with the habitual use of certain substances, including opiates. The chief physiological effects in question are generally agreed to be (1) tolerance, or the necessity for ever greater dosages of the substance to produce the original effect, and (2) the withdrawal syndrome, which is the onset of pronounced and uncomfortable physical symptoms when dosages of the substance are decreased or halted. Opium meets both of these criteria (tolerance and withdrawal, however, are also associated with a number of other substances including caffeine, nicotine, and alcohol). The rate of increase of tolerance and the kind and severity of withdrawal symptoms vary with individual users and circumstances, but the symptoms include, in the early stages (beginning four to six hours after the last dose), frequent yawning, sneezing, runny nose, and goose bumps and, in the later stages (twelve to seventy-two hours), violent diarrhea, alternating chills and sweats, hypersensitivity to touch, irritability and depression, and spontaneous orgasms. The psychological and social effects that are perhaps even more prominently constitutive of popular and professional notions of addiction, however, have always been significantly more difficult to pin to a consensus, and the choice of symptoms used to define addiction has historically depended on a series of factors having at least as much to do with institutional and cultural concerns as with supposedly physiological and psychological ones.

There is a dense network of interimplication spanning the development of addiction as a medical phenomenon, the rise of governmental control of opium sales, and the evolution of the medical professions in the latter quarter of the nineteenth century. The medical professions had evolved by leaps and bounds during the nineteenth century, largely by marking certain medical practices and practitioners as legitimate and then distinguishing them by means of legislation from ostensibly dangerous hacks and their quackery. At the beginning of the century, the rough equivalent to the domain of the modern general practitioner was divided among three types of medical professionals. From bottom to top in terms of prestige, they were (1) apothecaries, who were originally only dispensers of drugs but ultimately secured the legal prerogative also to prescribe, make house calls, and order treatments, as long as they did not charge for their services but only for the drugs they dispensed; (2) surgeons, who were systematically educated in anatomy, performed invasive operations, and treated with external medicines but were not legally entitled to prescribe internal medications; and (3) physicians, who were highly educated in the liberal arts but had only an unsystematic, ad hoc education in anatomy and other sciences, and who advised and prescribed for their patients rather than actually performing operations or hands-on treatments.[23]

Boundary disputes raged among the three orders and were especially heated between apothecaries and other vendors of drugs who did not fit neatly into any of the medical professional classifications. This gave rise to the Apothecaries' Act of 1815, which granted the Society of Apothecaries the right to examine and license apothecaries and denied the right to prescribe and sell certain medicines to anyone not so licensed (the Royal College of Surgeons and the Royal College of Physicians already had similar authority over their turfs). But there were still a number of widely used medicines that could be sold if not prescribed by any retailer, of which medicines opium is perhaps the most significant and representative. The continued availability, versatility, and inexpensiveness of opium meant a loss of potential business not only for apothecaries but also for physicians and surgeons, as a number of people simply bought their opium from their local publican, grocer, or tailor and treated themselves at home without ever consulting a medical professional.

In the 1860s, some physicians and surgeons began to advocate the new technology of the hypodermic injection of morphine (also known as morphia)[24] as an area of potentially exclusive expertise that would enable medical professionals to distinguish themselves in the public's eyes not only from a wide range of retailers but perhaps more importantly from the increasingly popular herbalists, hydropaths, and other "quacks" with whom physicians, surgeons, and apothecaries were forced to compete. Hypodermic injection greatly increased the efficacy of morphine and seemed at first to be almost a panacea. By 1870, however, some practitioners were warning that "injections of morphia, though free from the ordinary evils of opium eating, might, nevertheless, create the same artificial want and gain credit for assuaging a restlessness and depression of which it was itself the cause."[25]

As the 1870s progressed, European medical professionals began to define a new disease known primarily as morphinism or morphinomania, a series of symptoms associated with the prolonged hypodermic injection of morphine. Attention to this new disease was instigated in Britain by the translation of French and German treatises on the subject and was closely associated with debates about the treatment and legal control of alcoholism.[26] The treatment of addiction quickly emerged as a new medical specialty complete with its own experts, professional organizations, sanitoriums, and so forth. As in the cases of alcoholism, criminality, insanity, poverty, and homosexuality in the second half of the nineteenth century, the medical classification of morphinism as a disease tended to ignore social factors in favor of supposedly psychological and biological tendencies of the individual. Addiction, like all of the above, was a "disease of the will," as much a vice as an illness. The disease's connection to a larger social picture was emphasized in terms of effects rather than causes: it originated in the individual and his or her heredity, but it was taken as an indication of a general decline in the physical and moral health of Britons as a whole. Medical treatment tended to focus on the upper middle classes, who were presumed to have a "higher sensitiveness and greater vulnerability" to the disease, whereas working-class opiate use was viewed as a sort of generalized chronic intemperance rather than a specific disease.[27] The preferred means of dealing with working-class habitual use was not medical intervention but rather curtailment of supply. This bias was reflected in other institutional practices as well: middle-class habitual users tended to be treated in state-of-the-art sanitoriums while working-class users went to prison.

Even as doctors writing in such cutting-edge medical publications as the *Lancet* were decrying this "vicious habit" that was "undoubtedly a growing disease,"[28] the specialized medical literature on morphine addiction increasingly emphasized that the majority of cases originated in hypodermic injections, which, in accordance with the medical professional drive for exclusive control of the technology, were almost always either administered by medical professionals or self-administered by patients whom doctors had personally trained in the use of the needle. The irony of this seeming circularity was enhanced by the fact that the largest single group of habitual hypodermic morphine users was to be found within the medical professions themselves.

There also was little or no institutionalized distinction between medical and nonmedical or stimulant use (what now might be called recreational use) prior to the rise of the public health movement in the 1830s. Before the publication of De Quincey's *Confessions of an English Opium-Eater* (1821), the recreational use of opium had been represented only in terms of opium eating and smoking, both of which practices were supposed to be exclusively Oriental (indeed De Quincey's adoption of the adjective "English" was undoubtedly meant in part to preempt the implicit "Oriental" that would otherwise be attached to "Opium-Eater"). But the 1830s saw rising concern over opium poisonings (both accidental and deliberate), the practice of "infant doping," and the supposed stimulant use of opium among the working classes. The predominantly middle-class public health movement was most vocal about these supposed abuses, which were always tagged as working-class evils, and concern seems to have been motivated largely by the rising class tensions of an industrializing society ever more visibly and anxiously splitting into Disraeli's "two nations." This is not to say, however, that any of these condemned uses of opium was in fact confined to the working classes. Under any of the available criteria, for instance, De Quincey's practice of taking a dose of laudanum on Saturday nights to enhance his enjoyment of the opera should have conspicuously qualified as stimulant use. But his educated middle-class status apparently encouraged his also predominantly middle-class audience to place his recreational use in a different category than that of the Fenland or Lancashire laborer.

In addition to class sympathy, this tendency to excuse in De Quincey what was condemned in the laborer may have had roots in the belief that De Quincey's opium use enhanced his literary talents and was therefore justified by a means ostensibly unavailable to uneducated laborers. Such prejudices are by no means confined to the nineteenth century either. Alethea Hayter displays the same biases, for instance, when she pointedly distinguishes between "learned and brilliantly imaginative writers like Coleridge and De Quincey [who] saw fantastic visions under the influence of opium" and "uneducated unimaginative delinquents" who do not.[29] Berridge and Edwards more convincingly contend that the effects of opium on imaginative visions first described by De Quincey were neither exclusive nor original to himself or his class. Rather they "were widely known, but unrevealed because of 'cultural prejudices' and literary convention. The Romantic recognition of the value of imagination brought to the fore not new, but unspoken effects."[30] De Quincey himself was inconsistent vis-à-vis a class-based double standard. He embraced a decidedly hierarchical distinction between English and Oriental experiences of opium, questioning in the *Confessions* "whether any Turk, of all that ever entered the paradise of opium-eaters, can have had half the pleasure I had. But, indeed, I honour the Barbarians too much by supposing them capable of any pleasures approaching to the intellectual ones of an Englishman."[31] But he was more equivocal about differentiations between English opium eaters of different social classes. He famously proclaimed that "If a man whose talk is of oxen should become an opium-eater, the probability is that (if he is not too dull to dream at all)—he will dream of oxen." But class distinctions faded when he was justifying his habit on the basis of its wide practice, in which case both he and the "work-people" of Manchester were mutual members of the "class of opium-eaters," which was "a very numerous class indeed."[32] Both he and Cole-ridge, however, did associate working-class opium use with already available negative stereotypes about drunkenness. "The immediate occasion of [the prevalence of opium eating among the working classes]," said De Quincey, "was the lowness of wages, which, at that time, would not allow them to indulge in ale or spirits."[33] Coleridge similarly lamented that "the practice of taking opium is dreadfully spread—throughout Lancashire and Yorkshire it is the common dram of the lower order of people."[34]

But there is plenty of reason to believe that habitual opium use was common also among the middle classes. One need only scan the list of famous middle-class life-long users: the parliamentarian and premier abolitionist William Wilberforce, the pioneer photographer and son of the prestigious pottery baron Tom Wedgwood, the novelist Wilkie Collins, and poets George Crabbe and Francis Thompson. Known frequent users—who may or may not have been dependent at one time or another—include Keats,[35] Shelley, Byron, Scott, Elizabeth Barrett Browning, Jane Welsh Carlyle, and Dickens. Robert Clive, Indian imperialist extraordinaire, and Lizzie Siddal, artist and model of the Pre-Raphaelite circle, both died of opium poisoning and were widely presumed to have committed suicide. The supposedly working-class evil of infant doping was a frequent resort of middle-class parents as well, and numerous opium preparations such as Godfrey's Cordial and Mrs. Winslow's Soothing Syrup were prescribed for middle-class children by respected medical professionals throughout the century.

While debates over the opium trade raged within the houses of Parliament, they also carried on a sustained dialogue with popular culture. The anti-opium movement both borrowed from and influenced the popular press, for instance, with its alarmist representations of opium eating and smoking in *The Friend of China*. Both sides also consistently resorted to Coleridge and De Quincey as evidence either for or against the ill effects of habitual opium use, and those authors were themselves influenced by popular perceptions of Anglo-Oriental relations during the early days of the Indo-Chinese opium trade. Moralistic conceptions informed cultural productions dealing with opium as early as "Kubla Khan," and they were even more pronounced in late century, partly because of the combined activities of the anti-opium movement and the medical professions. When *The Friend of China* warned, for instance, that the British would someday suffer the consequences of their domineering treatment of China, this apprehension was both fuel for and evidence of anxieties about the increased influx of Chinese immigrants in the 1860s. These fears gained cultural currency in the latter half of the century, figuring prominently in the uneasy representations of opium dens in London's East End that appeared both inside and outside the overtly anti-opium press. And these cultural products completed the loop by feeding back into the legislative and institutional arenas. The magazine articles and fiction about opium dens are a case in point. All available evidence suggests that there were at most half a dozen informal dens in the East End at any one time, and those serving few or no English customers.[36] But despite the apparently extreme distortion of the popular accounts, the surgeon-major was nonetheless moved to declare to the British Medical Association in 1892 that the importance of eradicating the "opium-smoking saloons" in the East End "could not be overestimated."[37] The tenacity of the opium den myth has more to do with broad-based cultural dynamics—literary conventions, inherited assumptions about the Orient, imperialist anxieties, and fears of invasion—than with any activities that actually took place in London's East End.

National Identity

Nineteenth-century British fears and anxieties about opium and the Orient are intimately linked to the last term that needs contextualizing here, national identity. I invoke the term in reference to the sense of a generalized British character that was an increasingly prominent feature of late eighteenth- and nineteenth-century British discourse. The reasons for, and manifestations of, this increasing preoccupation with a unified national identity are complex and have been analyzed in some detail elsewhere,[38] but I will attempt a brief outline here. Two of the chief factors were the fact that Britain was at war for most of the latter half of the eighteenth century and the communications revolution that took place at the same time.[39] These factors met in the pro-war propaganda that proliferated amidst increasing tensions with France during the late eighteenth and early nineteenth centuries. As Stella Cottrell illustrates, pro-war broadsides represented a unified Britain as a family with a proud and noble lineage:

> "Briton" was a name with ancestry, worthy of recognition, and patriots fought to protect "our ancient name and character". Ancestral heroes, "our Edwards and Henries", provided a family genealogy for the whole nation. "These courageous men were Britons", ran one broadside; "We too are BRITONS. Let then all who claim that Title, and whose veins flow with BRITISH BLOOD, emulate the ardour, the courage, the glory of our Ancestors." Underlying this fetishisation of ancestors was an idealisation of continuity, which was glorified as a virtue and an achievement of itself. It was the fulcrum upon which the very notion of British identity turned. Continuity conferred legitimacy, it proved efficacy, it was the test of character.[40]

Such appeals to continuity were buttressed by the self-conscious contrasting of Britishness to other characters, the "particular construction of the external enemy . . . which, in every respect of character and social and political life, was the polar opposite of the British." [41] And the idea of a heroic, courageous, and unified British character proclaimed by the broadsides seemed in turn to be borne out by Britain's consistent military victories. As E. J. Hobsbawm argues, "a proven capacity for conquest" is one of the essential criteria for a sense of nationhood. "For the nineteenth century," he says, "conquest provided the Darwinian proof of evolutionary success as a social species." [42]

This is not to say, however, that the idea of a uniform British character took a comfortable and stable hold. Indeed the idea gained currency only in response to profound conflicts that it in many ways fueled rather than quelled. As Marlon Ross says, in the early nineteenth century,

> the British were confronted with the question of their country's relation to itself: its relation to its past menaced by the French Revolutionary zeal to begin anew, to abolish tradition; its relation to its borders menaced by Napoleon's empire-building, by its own conflictual desire to mimic Napoleon and to silence him, to enlarge its own borders but without losing its identity in relation to the exotic-external that defines its nationality. [43]

The Burkean metaphorical conception of the nation as a body both under-girded and undercut the idea of national integrity, Ross argues, as it came into conflict with another means of solidifying national identity, territorial expansion: "What is the difference between Napoleonic aggression, which disrupts the geographical integrity of the state's body, crushing independence abroad and liberty at home, and British expansion, which can be seen as integral growth, preordained by England's glorious past?" [44] Territorial expansion reinforces national identity by displaying its capacity for extension; but it simultaneously threatens that identity by blurring its center, rendering the very idea of "Britain" indeterminate by subsuming too many diverse regions and cultures to that name. Equally threatening is the international commerce that accompanies such expansion. As Ross says, "just at the point that the external-exotic must be absorbed in order for industry and trade to proceed apace, the nation is being defined as a harmonious, homogeneous living whole." [45] In other words, if you are what you eat, how can the nation-as-body be unequivocally British when it consistently consumes commodities that are not British?

It is at this point that opium becomes central, both as a metaphor for the dynamics of Anglo-Oriental exchange and as an actual commodity caught up in that exchange. The threat of Oriental commodities is significant enough when they are figuratively ingested into "British" culture, as in the cases of Persian rugs, Chinese porcelain, and japan-lacquered objets d'art. But when the foreign commodities in question are literally swallowed by individual British bodies, the figurative aspect of the threat is literalized. Tea, coffee, and many spices are examples of this phenomenon, but opium is perhaps the most broadly representative case, for not only was it literally ingested by British bodies (as were tea, spices, and so forth) but it also had a reputation for altering the consciousness of its user, and it is this dual force that prepares the ground for a cultural context in which to interpret opium and its attendant transformations as various forms of foreign invasion, invasions that are imagined in nineteenth-century British culture as simultaneously pleasurable and painful.

II

Pernicious Beverages

Coleridge, Opium, and Oriental Contamination

Everything about the Orient . . . exuded dangerous sex,
threatened hygiene and domestic seemliness with an exces-
sive "freedom of intercourse."

Edward
Said,
Orientalism

We cannot possibly interpret rituals concerning excreta,
breast milk, saliva and the rest unless we are prepared to
see in the body a symbol of society, and to see the powers
and dangers credited to social structures reproduced in
small on the human body.

Mary
Douglas,
Purity and
Danger

IN A PUBLIC lecture of 1795, Samuel Taylor Coleridge mounted a diatribe against British "commercial intercourse" in the Orient, focusing on the case of the East Indies as typical of the abuses he deplored:

> It has been openly asserted that our commercial intercourse with the East Indies has been the occasion of the loss of eight million Lives—in return for which most foul and heart-inslaving Guilt we receive gold, diamonds, silks, muslins & callicoes for fine Ladies and Prostitutes. Tea to make a pernicious Beverage, Porcelain to drink it from, and salt-petre for the making of gunpowder with which we may murder the poor Inhabitants who supply all these things.[1]

Among the many features that make this passage interesting is the subtle twist in its logical trajectory: although Coleridge appears at first to indict British commercial intercourse for its devastating effects upon East Indians, the development of his argument reveals that he is at least as concerned with the reverse, the effects of that intercourse upon Britons. For while he laments the loss of the eight million East Indian lives, he seems at least as troubled by the fact that these deaths have saddled England with a "most foul and heart-inslaving Guilt." Even the foulness he condemns is associated less explicitly with Britons' guilty actions than with the products of the commercial intercourse that serves as the "occasion" of those actions, for the pollution is linked most overtly with tainted Eastern commodities, the "pestilent Luxuries" that enter the British body politic and "leave an indelible stain on our national character."[2] This contaminative ingestion is illustrated most vividly by the centerpiece of Coleridge's list of contagious commodities, tea, whose purpose, he claims, is "to make a pernicious Beverage."

This image of a collective British body engaged in contaminative drinking appears often in Coleridge's writings, where it consistently figures fears of retribution for unsavory British behavior in the colonies. A letter to his brother is representative: "If it be God's will that the commercial Gourd should be canker-killed—if our horrible Iniquities in the W. India Islands & on the coasts of Guinea call for judgment on us—God's will be done!"[3] This recurrent scenario played out with respect to the collective English body has a more than metaphorical force when it involves Coleridge's individual body and its drinking of laudanum, a solution whose active ingredient is that substance so multifariously coded as Oriental, opium. This particular pernicious beverage has a comprehensive destabilizing effect on and around the individual body of the opium-eating author of "Kubla Khan," where it clouds the putative differentiations not only between English and Oriental, colonized and colonizer, but also between a series of binaries not as obviously correlating to opposed national counterparts, such as individual and collective, mother and child, male and female, rapist and victim, sacred and profane, and most encompassingly, self and other. These various unstable oppositions crosscut one another, yielding a pervasive instability of the individual's differentiation from any point of would-be contrasting reference, an effect to which Coleridge's response is itself unstable, for his reaction oscillates between attraction and repulsion, desire and dread, pleasure and pain, often encompassing what would seem to be polar opposites in the same moment.

Mother's Milk: "Fears in Solitude"

Both the prophetic tone and the specific imagery of Coleridge's exhortation against Anglo-Oriental commercial intercourse are also central to his poem "Fears in Solitude" (1797), which represents English commercial activity in the East as so much irresponsible drinking that can be expected to result in a sort of parallel to Montezuma's revenge: "We have drunk up, demure as at a grace," says the poet, "pollutions from the brimming cup of wealth" (lines 59–60).[4] The directionality of the contamination is implicitly reversed again as it was in the Bristol lecture, appearing at first to come from England but ultimately linking back to an implicit Oriental origin. The speaker argues that a seemingly imminent French invasion of English shores would be poetic justice for England's behavior toward its Eastern colonies, where

<blockquote>

(lines 41–43)

We have offended, Oh! my countrymen!
We have offended very grievously,
And been most tyrannous.
</blockquote>

He characterizes these despotic acts once again in terms of a deadly "taint" and "pestilence":

<blockquote>
From east to west
A groan of accusation pierces Heaven!

. . . . .

Like a cloud that travels on,
Steamed up from Cairo's swamps of pestilence,
Even so, my countrymen! have we gone forth
And borne to distant tribes slavery and pangs,
And, deadlier far, our vices, whose deep taint
With slow perdition murders the whole man,
His body and his soul!
</blockquote>

(lines 43–53)

Although the deadly colonial taint is associated most immediately with English "vices," the key simile of the passage diffuses culpability, establishing that these vices, though nominally English, find their defining precedent in Oriental scourges, for the taint is most like "a cloud . . . steamed up from Cairo's swamps of pestilence"—not fundamentally English but paradigmatically Oriental and contagious.

The drinking of contaminative foreign substances becomes the negative standard of comparison for pure British identity later in the poem as the speaker apostrophizes "dear Britain . . . my Mother Isle," proclaiming that

<blockquote>
from thy lakes and mountain-hills,
Thy clouds, thy quiet dales, thy rocks and seas,
[I] Have drunk in all my intellectual life.
</blockquote>

(lines 176, 184–86)

Because he drinks only from the quintessentially British body of this Mother Isle, he claims, "There lives nor form nor feeling in my soul / Unborrowed from my country" (lines 192–93). By framing pure national identity as a by-product of wholesome mother's milk, Coleridge indirectly takes part in an ongoing dispute over English childrearing customs. During the seventeenth century, middle-class English mothers had increasingly resorted to wet nurses, usually poor women who could be paid to assume the inconvenient task of breastfeeding middle-class infants. The practice gave rise to nervous anticipation that, as one writer put it, the nurses would "with their Milk . . . transfuse their Vices, and form in the Child such evil habits as will not easily be eradicated."[5] Such fears waned somewhat through the middle of the eighteenth century, but were in the ascendant again by the turn of the nineteenth.[6] The anxiety took on a national as well as a class bias in the Indian colonies, where many English mothers resorted to native wet nurses or *ammahs,* but not without a nagging fear that, as one guidebook for colonial wives put it later in the century, "milk of 'native women' might contaminate an English child's character."[7]

It is tempting to see Coleridge as reiterating such conflation of purity and Englishness in his metaphor of mother's milk, for it is easy to imagine him portraying England as the good mother who nurses her children with a pure soul-nurturing milk while casting the Orient as the bad mother who serves up a rancid and character-degrading pernicious beverage. But the poem's proposition that mother's milk is tantamount to intellectual influence causes the dichotomy to play out not quite so conveniently, for rather than opposing the intellectual influences of England and the Orient, Coleridge instead describes them as having initially shaped his personality in much the same way: both fostered his ability to apprehend a metaphysical unity. The nutritional breakdown of the "intellectual life" he has "drunk in" from his Mother Isle includes

(lines 187–91)
> All sweet sensations, all ennobling thoughts,
> All adoration of the God in nature,
> All lovely and all honourable things,
> Whatever makes this mortal feel
> The joy and greatness of its future being.

But he elsewhere attributes the nurturance of this same sublime imagination to his childhood reading of Oriental tales: "from my early reading of Faery Tales & Genii &c &c—my mind had been habituated *to the Vast*—& I never regarded *my senses* in any way as the criteria of my belief."[8] While both the English and Oriental influences foster a heightened sense of the metaphysical, the Oriental influence also fosters an ambivalently charged emphasis on the physical: "At six years old I remember to have read . . . the Arabian Nights' entertainments," says Coleridge in another letter of the period, ". . . and I distinctly remember the anxious & fearful eagerness with which I used to watch the window, in which the books lay—& whenever the Sun lay upon them, I would seize it, carry it by the wall, & bask & read." This piece of bildungsroman, with its protagonist guiltily sneaking off to a corner to indulge in forbidden pleasures, reads as much like a confession of masturbation as a celebration of intellectual growth, and his clergyman father responded much as if it had been the former: he "found out the effect, which these books had produced—and burnt them."[9] The downright sensual pleasure of reading the Oriental tales blurs the distinction between intellectual influence and physical affect, between the reader's body and the text he reads. Consistent with then current fears of the degenerative effects of masturbation or "self-pollution," Coleridge's reminiscences dwell on the enervating effects his secret Orientalist reading exercised upon both body and intellect: "I became a *dreamer,* and acquired an indisposition to all bodily activity—and I was fretful, and inordinately passionate, and as I could not play at any thing, and was slothful, I was despised & hated by the boys." [10] In addition to making him sensual and lazy, the young Coleridge's Orientalist reading apparently compromised his masculinity.

This Orientally induced neurasthenia reaches its peak with the adult Coleridge's irresistible attraction to an ad hoc conglomeration of quasi-Oriental elements he dubs "the Brahman Creed." Writing of his poem "This Lime-Tree Bower My Prison," he laments that "it is but seldom that I raise & spiritualize my intellect to this height—& at other times I adopt the Brahman Creed, & say—It is better to sit than to stand, it is better to lie than to sit, it is better to sleep than to wake—but Death is the best of all!" The sense of vastness that was elsewhere the Orient's most positive influence on his intellectual and spiritual development here implies its own negation, becoming the most profound possible contrast to raising and spiritualizing the intellect. Whereas he once "[knew] no other way of giving the mind a love of 'the Great' and 'the Whole,'" the quasi-Oriental sensibility he shorthands as the Brahman Creed is now the despairing refuge of a mind to which "*all things* appear little—all the knowledge that can be acquired, child's play—the universe itself—what but an immense heap of *little* things?"

The negating capacity of the Brahman Creed verges into a thanatopic principle as the impulses it shorthands drive toward a death as prebirth. Coleridge continues, "I should much wish, like the Indian Vishna to float about along an infinite ocean cradled in the flower of the Lotos, & wake once in a million years for a few minutes—just to know that I was going to sleep a million years more." [11] The scene with its projected sleeper rocking within the cradle of the Oriental lotus on the infinite ocean encodes the Orient again as a rival mother to the English one; the would-be seafaring slumberer desires to return not to the lakes and seas of his English Mother Isle, but to the womblike cradle of the lotus on the infinite ocean of the Orient. His desire to recoup this Oriental womb is an ambivalent one, though, for while the concomitant oblivion has considerable appeal, it is also the very factor he was to cite again and again throughout his life as the downfall that has become a persistent cliché among Coleridge biographers: the lure of inactivity that drew him from ostensibly worthy pursuits and was the focus of intense feelings of guilt—a guilt that is explicitly associated in other instances with his opium addiction.

This retrogressive desire to return to the womb is predictably focused at other moments on the English Mother Isle. The speaker of "Fears in Solitude" drinks not only from breast-like "mountain-hills," but also from a more inclusive feminized body/landscape, featuring archetypally womblike "lakes" and "seas" as well as "quiet dales."[12] While the speaker's pleasurable physical engagements with a feminized English landscape are also interpretable as understated sexual impulses toward the Mother Isle, they are not the guilty ones associated with the young Coleridge's attraction to the Orient. Instead the speaker sees this overwhelming desire to be within the Mother Isle as part and parcel of his joyfully comprehensive and unequivocally holy "natural love" for England, which he proclaims proudly rather than indulging guiltily in a corner:

(lines
176–81)

> O dear Britain! O my Mother Isle!
> Needs must thou prove a name most dear and holy
> To me, a son, a brother, and a friend,
> A husband, and a father! who revere
> All bonds of natural love, and find them all
> Within the limits of thy rocky shores.

The mere memory of this feminized landscape has an ennobling effect:

(lines
228–32)

> Remembering thee, O green and silent dell!
> . . . all my heart
> Is softened, and made worthy to indulge
> Love, and the thoughts that yearn for human kind.

His presence inside this figurative female body might be interpreted as either sexual penetration or an alternative realization of the prebirth scenario he pursued through his imaginative encounter with the Brahman Creed. Either way, while the oceanic Oriental womb is a sanctuary of restful inertia and oblivion, the hills and dales of the Mother Isle are the site of energetic intellectual and emotional engagement. Thus, in order to enjoy the seductive inertia of the Oriental infinite ocean, Coleridge must dissociate himself from the galvanizing influence of the lakes and seas of his Mother Isle, from which he has drunk in all his intellectual life. And he does turn away from this figurative mother's milk to drink instead a pernicious beverage, the milk of the rival Oriental mother.

The Milk of Paradise: "Kubla Khan"

The story told by the preface to "Kubla Khan" is at least as familiar as the poem itself: after having taken "two grains of opium,"[13] the author says, he was reading in what he calls *Purchas's Pilgrimage* (1614) about the palace of Kublai Khan, founder of the Mongol dynasty in China, when he fell into a deep sleep and saw before him the turbulent and paradisal Oriental landscape he attempts to

recreate through the verse of "Kubla Khan." This terrain too is initially feminized, centering around the genital-like "deep romantic chasm which slanted /
Down the green hill athwart a cedarn cover" (lines 12–13). But the temperament of the Oriental landscape-body is far from the silent stillness of its English
counterpart; it is instead

(lines 14–16)
>A savage place! as holy and enchanted
>As e'er beneath a waning moon was haunted
>By woman wailing for her demon-lover.

In fact it is wildly, even dangerously orgasmic:

(lines 17–22)
>From this chasm, with ceaseless turmoil seething,
>As if the earth in fast thick pants were breathing,
>A mighty fountain momently was forced:
>Amid whose swift, half-intermitted burst
>Huge fragments vaulted like rebounding hail,
>Or chaffy grain beneath the thresher's flail.

Instead of presenting its fluids passively as lakes and seas from which the
poet might sip peacefully at his leisure, this landscape forces forth "a mighty
fountain" that threatens to engulf all that lies in its path. Although the eruption
originates in the feminized romantic chasm, the flow forced forth in "swift,
half-intermitted burst" is at best ambiguously gendered, hearkening perhaps
more readily to seminal emission than to late eighteenth-century understand-
ings of female ejaculation. Such ambiguously gendered fluids also play a key
role in the portion of Purchas's book Coleridge claims to have been reading
when he dozed:

>Cublai Can . . . *hath a Heard or Drove of Horses and Mares, about ten thou-
>sand, as white as snow; of the milke whereof none may taste, except he be of
>the bloud of* Cingis Can. . . . *According to the direction of his Astrologers or
>Magicians, he on the eight and twentieth day of August aforesaid, spendeth and
>poureth forth with his owne handes the milke of these Mares in the ayre, and
>on the earth, to give drink to the spirits and Idols which they worship, that they
>may preserve the men, women, beasts, birds, corne, and other things growing
>on the earth.* [14]

Purchas's diction as he has Kubla "spendeth and poureth forth with his owne
handes the milke . . . in the ayre, and on the earth" is strongly reminiscent of a
narrative contemporary with his own, the King James Version of the Bible's
account of Onan's punishment for ejaculating on the ground, a parallel that, in
conjunction with the sacred liquid's mystified fertilizing capacity, reinforces the

latent suggestion that the milk is also akin to semen.[15] For a mere mortal—and not even a Tartar, let alone a kinsman of Genghis Khan—to drink this potent liquid would be to transgress the sacred laws that govern the Oriental domain. It would also be to ingest at the same time the fertile life force of the East against which he has transgressed. In other words, for the speaker to drink this milk is both to commit a crime and to plant in himself the seeds of his would-be punisher at the same time.

The introduction of this highly charged fluid into the poet's body is also credited with giving rise to the poem, for his visionary demonization is imputed in the final line to his having drunk "the milk of Paradise." As the critical legacy of "Kubla Khan" indicates, it is almost impossible not to equate this milk of Paradise with the laudanum to which the preface attributes the poem's spontaneous composition.[16] Being both Oriental commodity and milk of Paradise, laudanum plays the role of milk from an Oriental body, thus indirectly realizing the aforementioned cultural anxieties surrounding Oriental women's wet-nursing English children as it orientalizes the drinker's consciousness.[17] In a similar sense, laudanum also plays out the retribution scenario Coleridge warned against in his Bristol lecture and "Fears in Solitude," for to ingest opium is literally to consume an Oriental commodity, and thus, extending Coleridge's own logic, it is to perpetuate and share in the guilty taint of the larger national shame of exploiting the Orient while at the same time dangerously allowing, even inviting that understandably vindictive Orient to enter the English body in both its individual and collective forms. To drink laudanum is thus symbolically to incur guilt for the Anglo-Oriental commercial intercourse and its punishment at one quaff.

Running parallel to this current of ambiguously gendered and gendering fluids in "Kubla Khan" is the attempt enacted at every level to tame and contain the vast, evasive, and potentially obliterative forces of the Oriental landscape and the sexuality associated with it. Within the poem, Kubla himself decrees that "twice five miles of fertile ground / with walls and towers [be] girdled round" (lines 6–7), and he succeeds in rendering Xanadu a passive and benevolent landscape like Coleridge's Mother Isle insofar as his enclosures contain a few quiet dales of their own, "gardens bright with sinuous rills" and "sunny spots of greenery."[18] "But Oh!," in the second verse paragraph the landscape bursts fiercely through its containment with the explosive orgasm of the deep romantic chasm. What then ensues is a metaphorical sexual intercourse between partners of surrealistically blurred genders: the phallic mighty fountain emerges from the notably nonphallic chasm, and the fluids from the chasm then enter other caverns, flowing in a "sacred river" through "caverns measureless to man" only to sink ultimately "in tumult to a lifeless ocean" reminiscent of the womblike infinite ocean previously associated with the Brahman Creed.[19] The scene seems at first glance to be a positive liberation as it enables a release of sexual energy and the possibility of escape from rigidly demarcated gender roles. But the end result is a nihilistic Armageddon: the womblike "sunless sea" within the measureless caverns is not a source of life but is instead conspicuously "lifeless"; and "'mid this tumult Kubla heard from far / Ancestral voices prophesying war!" (lines 5, 28–30). Kubla's attempt at containment, then, not only fails but also precipitates a violent reaction with overtones of retribution against the arrogant emperor who dared aspire to tame these powerful forces.

Another version of Kubla's failed enclosure is attempted at the level of the poem's composition, according to the narrative told jointly by its final verse paragraph and its preface, and this metacontainment ultimately yields results with similarly retributive overtones. The preface recounts that the substance of the poem spontaneously exploded into the author's consciousness: "all the images rose up before him as *things,* with a parallel production of the correspondent expressions, without any sensation or consciousness of effort." But after the initial eruption, the waves of images attenuated, leaving only a frustratingly calm surface like that of the "lifeless ocean": "with the exception of some eight or ten scattered lines and images, all the rest had passed away like the images on the surface of a stream into which a stone has been cast." This explosion and attenuation pattern is recapitulated within the poem when the pyrotechnic description of Xanadu halts abruptly only to give way to a nostalgic account like the preface's of the spontaneous appearance and disappearance of the vision that inspired the poem. Like Kubla Khan's landscape, this founding vision is tellingly configured as a mysterious and powerful Oriental woman, an "Abyssinian maid" who invades the speaker's consciousness and controls his vision, leading him to question whether "that indeed can be called composition in which all the images rose up before him as *things,*" as he says in the preface. By imputing inspiration and control of the poem's production to an independent-willed Oriental woman within his consciousness, the speaker partitions that consciousness into male and female, English and Oriental, demonic and docile, then reimagines the seemingly uncontrollable portions as something other than himself—specifically as the at least doubly other (both non-English and nonmale) Oriental woman. But the alien pieces remain, or at least return periodically, to erode the otherwise presumed stable center of his identity as, among other things, Englishman.

But, if the speaker fears and resents the identity-eroding intrusion of these volatile "other" elements, he also desires that intrusion for the power it provides despite (or perhaps because of) the submission and humiliation it entails. He declares his desire to be reinvaded by the Oriental woman, but couches it in active terms of containing and controlling rather than a passive diction of invasion. "Could I revive within me / Her symphony and song," he says, then he would be able not only to describe the elusive Oriental landscape he saw in his vision but actually to manifest it for others:

> I would build that dome in air
> (lines 46–48)   That sunny dome! those caves of ice!
> And all who heard should see them there.

His fantasy is to capture this Oriental woman who spontaneously invaded his consciousness before, but this time submit her to *his* control rather than endure the artistically emasculating process of composing by proxy for a feminized Orient. But intersecting this containment fantasy—perhaps competing with it, perhaps reinforcing it—is a desire to theatricalize his previous possession by the Oriental woman, to make of it a spectacle by which he can arouse not only himself but others as well. Evidence for both desires is the very existence of "Kubla Khan," which attempts to recreate and marshal the vision within a structure of the poet's own creation, but which also draws attention to, even revels in its own failure in that attempt.

These conflicting drives toward on the one hand a controlling containment and on the other hand invasion are echoed in Coleridge's attitude toward a character in another work from the same period, again a powerful Oriental woman, the Moorish Alhadra in his verse tragedy *Osorio*. When Coleridge speaks in the aforementioned letter of his desire to embrace the Brahman Creed, he adds that "I have put this feeling in the mouth of Alhadra, my Moorish Woman."[20] He thus reverses the process described in "Kubla Khan," as it is he who puts the words and images into the mouth of the Oriental woman rather than vice versa. But even when he creates an Oriental woman and tries to yoke her to a specific purpose, it is still she who seems to be in control, for her voice appears to usurp the discourse in which she is quoted and bend it to different ends, speaking not only of her Brahman Creed (a desire "to float for ever with a careless course") but also—and more emphatically—of her vindictive tendencies, "this deep contempt for all things / which quenches my revenge!" (350). In the context of *Osorio*, Alhadra also proves to be much more the voice of an oppressed and revenge-seeking Orient than of the serene and docile Brahman Creed.[21] She cites the very "law of Mahomet" as "The deep and stubborn purpose of revenge" (586), and in a long soliloquy that closes the play, she thanks Heaven for the "misery which makes the oppressed man / Regardless of his own life," and thus "makes him too / Lord of the oppressor's." She revels in the belief that, "Knew I an Hundred men / Despairing, but not palsied by despair, / This arm should shake the kingdoms of this world," and "The strong holds of the cruel men should fall" (596–97).

By speaking through—or being spoken through by—Alhadra, Coleridge once again elides the differences between male and female, England and Orient, but he adds to the list of blurred distinctions with the one between oppressor and oppressed. The "cruel men" of *Osorio* are the Spaniards who dominate the Moors, while the oppressors who preoccupy the author of "Fears in Solitude" and the Bristol lectures are the English who have "borne to distant tribes slavery and pangs." But becoming increasingly relevant here is a third pairing: the author and the representations he creates. For as we have been seeing, the author of "Kubla Khan" and *Osorio* is preoccupied with the assimilation and control of the Orient of his representations. As Alhadra speaks for an oppressed Orient that will rise up against its oppressors, then, she also highlights that this feminized Orient's ability to usurp the author's discourse and consciousness has more dire implications than just loss of artistic control. For the Englishman-author, to contain this irrepressible and vindictive Orient, whether by choice or by being invaded, is to risk being obliterated when it inevitably erupts, destroying its bonds.

Thirst of Revenge

As I have indicated, opium was both the most threatening and the most representative commodity with respect to notions of Oriental invasion through ingestion. If tea was a pernicious Oriental beverage, as Coleridge inveighed in his Bristol lecture, then laudanum, a solution of opium and alcohol, was even more of one: apart from being culturally coded and even mystified as an Oriental substance, opium was acknowledged as capable of altering consciousness, and it mirrored in nightmarish, almost parodic proportions Coleridge's fear of Britain's appetitive consumerism with its tendency to incite its user to ingest ever greater quantities until his or her consciousness and body were radically altered. When these peculiar properties of opium are combined with the idea that the Orient is infiltrating Britain through the tainted commodities Britons ingest, the drug frighteningly emerges as the Oriental commodity most able to introduce a vindictive, consciousness-usurping Orient into the British body and mind and to convert them from British to Oriental.

It is not surprising, then, that Coleridge's increasing consumption of laudanum in the late 1790s awakened in him fears and vivid images of his own personal Oriental invasion. From the beginning of his usage, he thought of opium as a mighty conquering and occupying force, though initially with positive effects. In a letter written early in his relationship with the drug, he writes of laudanum as a military power superior to the invading army of pain: "I took between 60 & 70 drops of Laudanum, and . . . On Friday [the pain] only *niggled;* as if the Chief had departed as from a conquered place, and merely left a small garrison behind."[22] But such positive images gradually yielded to negative ones until Coleridge was persistently wracked by torturous opium dreams of violent invaders come to punish him for some unspeakable crime. In one incident of 1800, the invader was again a powerful Oriental woman in "a most frightful Dream of a Woman whose features were blended with darkness catching hold of my right eye & attempting to pull it out . . . the Woman's name [was] Ebon Ebon Thalud."[23] Later, in "The Pains of Sleep" (1803), opium dreams supply greater numbers of even more ferocious invaders, a "fiendish crowd / Of shapes and thoughts that tortured me," a "trampling throng" harboring a "thirst of revenge" for some "intolerable wrong" (lines 16–21). The pained dreamer confounds guilt and suffering, oppressing and being oppressed, pleasure and pain, as he finds "desire with loathing strangely mixed" and grapples with a diffuse consciousness of

(lines 27–32)

> Deeds to be hid which were not hid,
> Which all confused I did not know
> Whether I suffered or I did:
> For all seemed guilt, remorse, or woe,
> My own or others' still the same
> Life-stifling fear, soul-stifling shame.

This confused invasion and the ambivalent feelings it evokes are in many ways reminiscent of the consciousness-invading vision of "Kubla Khan," an impression reinforced by the fact that, when Coleridge finally published "Kubla Khan" in 1816, he put "The Pains of Sleep" alongside it, introducing it in the preface as "a fragment . . . describing with equal fidelity the dream of pain and disease."

This dangerous internalization of the Orient does have potentially positive effects on the art of the visionary poet of "Kubla Khan," for it is his ingestion of a concentrated Orient in the form of the milk of Paradise that he believes would allow him to manifest the Oriental scene for an audience, causing it presumably to sprout forth from him after he has drunk the Orient's essence or seed. But this artistic enhancement comes at a high price, for not only does it entail allowing a hostile alien into his body it also risks incurring the alienative wrath of his own community. The poet believes a renewed occupation by the Abyssinian maid would enable him to elevate his audience to a frenzied emotional pitch, thus allowing him to experience the intoxicating power of the visionary, but he also anticipates that this roused audience would turn its fervor against him with all the fear and suspicion appropriate to a plague, treating him as an unclean, unholy, and potentially infectious pariah:

(lines 49–54)

> And all should cry, Beware! Beware!
> His flashing eyes, his floating hair!
> Weave a circle round him thrice,
> And close your eyes with holy dread,
> For he on honey-dew hath fed,
> And drunk the milk of Paradise.

This milk-and-honey-drenched derangement is, as Elisabeth Schneider points out, a version of the classical model of poetic inspiration, the possession of the poet by the muse as described by Plato:

> *All good poets, epic as well as lyric, compose their beautiful poems not by art but because they are inspired and possessed. And as the Corybantian revellers when they dance are not in their right mind, so the lyric poets are not in their right mind when they are composing their beautiful strains: but when falling under the power of music and metre they are inspired and possessed; like Bacchic maidens who draw milk and honey from the rivers when they are under the influence of Dionysus but not when they are in their right mind.[24]*

To be possessed by the muse, then, is also to be feminized, to be "like Bacchic maidens," and the feminine force of this Dionysian possession is often figured as a destructive one for the Greeks, as when a group of bacchic maidens tears Pentheus to pieces and marches on the city in Euripides's *The Bacchae*.[25] The fear the speaker projects onto his audience is perhaps an inheritance of this Hellenic anxiety as well as apprehension with respect to a potential repetition of the scenario he has outlined through both Kubla's disastrous landscaping efforts and his own similar self-destructive attempts to harness the Oriental muse: the feminine force possessing the poet, as Coleridge portrays it, can be expected to burst its bonds and flow outward from the point of eruption, and this volcanic center in Coleridge's scenario is none other than the poet who would, through his own explosion, disseminate the influence that inspired him and altered his identity, threatening to alter others as well. So the laudanum that supposedly catalyzed the vision is also the milky seed of the Orient is also the distilled essence of poetic inspiration, the Dionysian milk and honey flowing from the classical lyric muse. The ostracism that attends the poet's vision is thus both the honorific badge of the poet and the quarantine of the Typhoid Mary of Orientalism.

It is tempting to equate the poet's projected audience in "Kubla Khan" with a common interpretation of Coleridge's Britain as a repressive patriarchal colonial order[26] and to construe his anticipation of that community's negative response as a comment upon and a revision of a patriarchal model of imperialism. Coleridge, such an interpretation might say, expects the imperialistic order to recoil as the feminine sexuality/Orient it has tried both to contain and assimilate peeps through the bars with flashing eyes, threatening to burst out of its cage, which is both the body of the poet and, by extension, that patriarchal order itself. The structure and content of "Kubla Khan," in which the powerful feminine force bursts through and obliterates the feeble male bonds that shackle it, would thus recapitulate and reinforce the audience's fear.

D. A. Miller speaks of a similar phenomenon, "the 'origins' of male nervousness in female contagion," enacted later in the century, when "male security . . . seems always to depend on female claustration." The men Miller describes are secure as long as the feminine seems to be contained, but not if it is contained within themselves, for that uncomfortably complicates their sense of their own gender roles. Occupation by the female is further terrifying to these men because, Miller argues, it also resembles but inverts a classic rape scenario, of which "the most important fantasy feature . . . is the reaffirmation of the rapist's unimpaired capacity to withdraw, the integrity of his body (if not his victim's) recovered intact."[27] This inverted rape has much in common with Coleridge's Oriental possession, for the Orient also plays the role of the rapist thus configured. Although Coleridge's Orient is often feminized, it is at other times phallic, entering the poet's similarly ambiguous male/female body and displaying its power over that body, destructively (pleasurably?) altering it instead of vice versa. Kubla's bonds, the poet, and the poet's fearful community similarly play the roles of both victim and victimizer, trying to contain, tame, and alter the volatile Orient but also being penetrated and altered, perhaps even destroyed by that Orient, which is also both victim and victimizer, male and female.

This partially inverted rape scenario (partial because the roles are ambiguous rather than clearly reversed) is in turn a partial reversal of the colonial one Coleridge consistently indicted in which England has entered and destructively altered the Orient.[28] But it would be too simple to say that "Kubla Khan" represents Coleridge's punishment for his implicit participation in colonial atrocities, for it ultimately disables the very distinctions between parties that would lend meaning to such a directional process. The poem blurs boundaries between male and female, English and Oriental, victim and oppressor, as Oriental potentate and English poet alike attempt to contain the initially feminized Orient but in the process are themselves penetrated and altered by an Orient that in turn has become implicitly masculine at the moment of penetration. The narrative constituted by the poem and its preface mirrors Coleridge's sense of the colonial scenario he previously indicted, in which England has entered and destructively altered the Orient but has also caused the Orient to enter and destructively alter England. But the invasive Orient not only leaves "an indelible stain on our national character," it ultimately disables any definition of that character, finally rendering it indistinguishable from the Oriental (or any other supposed national character, for that matter). For England is arguably cast as a rapist when it destructively penetrates the Orient but is more like a classic conception of the victim when the Mother Isle is penetrated by destructive Oriental commodities. Thus the infection transmitted through contaminative nursing is also a venereal one transmitted by means of a polluting "commercial intercourse"; the fluid that was feminized as rancid mother's milk is also masculinized as infectious semen, and the intercourse by which it is transmitted configures each party as both rapist and victim. The gender of these entities is impossible to pinpoint, and so finally are their nationalities, their individual identities, their very physical differentiation from one another, for both England and the Orient ultimately occupy the same body under the influence of opium.

III

"The Causes of My Horror Lie Deep"

De Quincey, Opium, and the Excavated Oriental Origins of British Identity

FOR COLERIDGE, as we have seen, opium enables the Orient to take shape in his English consciousness, and that intrusion is for him tantamount to an invasion bent on avenging English exploitation. But the Oriental dream presence also arises from and reinforces his life-long engagement with a fantasized version of the Orient. This engagement is itself both pleasurable and painful: Coleridge views it as central to the formation of his Romantic consciousness and celebrates it as such, but he also perceives it as compromising a number of definitional divisions that inform his sense of identity: English/Oriental, male/female, and most basically, self/other. Many of the same tensions permeate the prose of Coleridge's sometime admirer and fellow opium habitué, Thomas De Quincey, whose literary oeuvre is also steeped in his Orientalesque opium visions. As one critic has said, "the most intense accounts of De Quincey's opium-induced nightmares in the *Confessions* seem to emulate the visionary Orientalism of *Kubla Khan* but render it horrible by organizing it around the self-tormenting psychic divisions of *The Pains of Sleep*."[1] This characterization is helpful in so far as it identifies "psychic divisions" as the key to the dreams' disturbing quality. But to call that disturbance "self-tormenting" is both to home in on its most significant aspect and to miss its point at the same time, for such a formulation assumes a stable self that does the tormenting, when in fact it is the radical instability of the self, the nagging sense that divisions never hold, that underlies De Quincey's torment at its most basic level. As he said in proto-Derridean terms in the *Confessions*, "it may be observed generally that, wherever two thoughts stand related to each other by a law of antagonism, and exist, as it were, by mutual repulsion, they are apt to suggest each other" (111).[2] It is this pattern of implosive binaries that permeates De Quincey's conception of the self, which necessarily always suggests whatever other it is defined against. To speak of De Quincey's dreams as "self-tormenting," then, is to beg the question that seems to be at the heart of the torment to begin with: that is, where does the self end and the other begin?[3]

De Quincey attempts to answer this fundamental question by looking inward, searching for a stable center to the self within his own consciousness. But, as in his Piranesian dreams of climbing staircase after staircase only to reach yet another staircase, that supposedly stable center is at best always on the horizon, never coming any closer. At worst, he discovers the opposite of a stable center: "The dreamer finds housed within himself—occupying, as it were, some separate chamber in his brain—holding, perhaps, from that station a secret and detestable commerce with his own heart—some horrid alien nature" (*CW,* 13:291).[4] De Quincey's opium dreams are so torturous precisely because they erode the desired division between self and other even in the otherwise presumably inviolate sanctum of individual consciousness.

De Quincey's favored means of provisionally conceptualizing this division is to cast the familiar term as the West and the alien one as the East. The skeleton of this paradigm is articulated by his "translation" of "Kant on National Character in Relation to the Sense of the Sublime and the Beautiful," an essay that attempts to clarify the concept of national character by opposing Western or European characters, those found in "our quarter of the globe," to Oriental ones, those indigenous to "other quarters of the world." But the assumed geographical boundary turns out to be more a mirror than a dividing wall when Persians emerge as "the Asiatic Frenchmen," Arabs "the Asiatic Spaniards," and Japanese "the Englishmen of the Oriental world" (*CW,* 14:53–55). De Quincey speaks similarly in the *Confessions* of "the barrier of utter abhorrence, and want of sympathy, placed between us [Asia and Englishmen] by feelings deeper than I can analyze" (109), but the occasion for even mentioning this "barrier" is an elaborate demonstration of what is implied in the Kant essay: that it is in fact not a barrier at all. What is supposed to lie on its other side instead manifests itself full-blown in the opium eater's consciousness when the internalized "horrid alien nature" takes the form of "the unimaginable horror . . . of Oriental imagery and mythological tortures" in his opium dreams. He is "transported into Asiatic scenes" without leaving his English cottage, and his identity ultimately disintegrates as he lies "confounded with all unutterable slimy things, amongst reeds and Nilotic mud" (109).

John Barrell argues that De Quincey attempts to limit such intersections between European and Oriental by thinking of each internal manifestation of the Orient as a case of infection and then searching for a way of protecting himself against it. The means upon which he most often settles, according to Barrell, is a version of what was then the cutting-edge medical technology for combating infection: inoculation. De Quincey's version of inoculation consists of "taking something of the East into himself, and projecting whatever he could not acknowledge as his out into a further East, an East *beyond* the East."[5] But there is a potentially fatal contradiction inherent within all inoculation, for it "involves simultaneously protecting someone against a disease and infecting them with it," and "there was no guarantee that he might not rediscover [the feared] disorder in the East he had taken in as well as in the East he had thrown away."[6] Barrell goes on to deconstruct De Quincey's various models of inoculation, showing that each is doomed to failure because the opium eater repeatedly reinforces the infection by the very means with which he seeks to conquer it. What Barrell stops one step short of saying, however, is that De Quincey's fight against Oriental infection by any means is doomed to failure because it has in fact misidentified the problem. The infection hypothesis presupposes that the two bodies were once separate, even if they are now inextricably intertwined in what Barrell calls "a *hybrid* identity." As we shall see, however, De Quincey's prose repeatedly arrives at the implicit conclusion that the two entities never were separate, that the most other, ultimate East did not ever actually enter his body, consciousness, or even his country, but was instead always there to begin with, for it turns out in the final analysis to be the origin of all things British and indeed of all Western culture in general.[7]

This idea of the Orient as all-encompassing origin was a common one in De Quincey's day (it was, among other things, the backbone of the German Higher Criticism of the Bible that so captured Coleridge's imagination), and such arguments were no doubt familiar to De Quincey, who took pride in his wide reading. But the Oriental origin in those contexts always functions implicitly as something forever buried in the untouchably distant past, a lost abstraction overwritten by, for instance, the proud heroic tradition of British identity. In De Quincey's dreams, however, opium exhumes the Oriental, which proves to have been not so deeply buried after all, and renders it a formidable force that tears apart the very notion of British identity in the present. The corrosive potential of the Orient lies chiefly in its protean ability to function as the crucial term in two distinct paradigms of British identity at once, paradigms that are supposed to be complementary but instead emerge as contradictory under the scrutiny of an opium-induced consciousness. On one hand, the Orient is the other against which British identity is contrasted. But, on the other hand, the Orient is also the primordial source of the tradition with which Britishness is supposed to be continuous. So, if the Orient is the source of the British tradition, and if Britons are, as one nationalist broadside proclaimed, "IMMUTA-BLY THE SAME,"[8] then the British character is paradoxically also its own opposite, the Oriental character.

It seems an irreconcilable paradox that, although De Quincey brands the exposure of the alien nature within the self "a curse too mighty to be sustained," he nonetheless courts it repeatedly by ingesting the opium that instigates the dreams in which the internal alien steps into the light. And, contrary to his own assertion, these "anarchical horrors" do anything but "gloomily [retire] from exposition" (*CW,* 13:292). Instead they aggressively come forward again and again in his prose—most notably in the *Confessions of an English Opium Eater,* "The English Mail-Coach," and "Suspiria de Profundis," which I will examine in the rest of this chapter. These and other De Quincey essays repeatedly outline hierarchical divisions between East and West, inside and outside, self and other, only to invert the hierarchies and blur the divisions in processes closely associated with the use of opium. By effortlessly moving the devalued other term from the bottom to the top, De Quincey implies that bottom and top, self and other, are interchangeable, that the spectrum of difference is not a line but a circle, that what lies at the farthest end of the spectrum necessarily comes full circle back to the near end. That which is most other to the self on De Quincey's continuum paradoxically also *is* the self, the outside *is* the inside, the "horrid alien nature" is "housed within himself," and what Barrell calls the "East *beyond* the East" rounds the globe to become West again—or worse yet, to expose that West always was East to begin with.

A Revolution of a Chinese Character

Although De Quincey characterizes his typically digressive essay "The English Mail-Coach" (1849, rev. 1854) as a meditation on the relationship between formative experiences and dreams, it is in fact as much about unstable boundaries of identity, a concern illustrated through its various inside/outside dichotomies. One of the first sidetracks on the road toward the concluding virtuosic "Dream-Fugue" is a lengthy digression on the set of "bye-laws . . . enacted by the inside passengers for the illustration of their own haughty exclusiveness":

(*CW,* 13:273)

> *Up to this time, say 1804, or 1805 (the year of Trafalgar), it had been the fixed assumption of the four inside people (as an old tradition of all public carriages derived from the reign of Charles II) that they, the illustrious quaternion, constituted a porcelain variety of the human race, whose dignity would have been compromised by exchanging one word of civility with the three miserable delf-ware outsides. Even to have kicked an outsider might have been held to attaint the foot concerned in that operation, so that, perhaps, it would have required an act of Parliament to restore its purity of blood.*

For the passengers who ride inside, the inside/outside division is a microcosm of English social hierarchy, with themselves cast as the upper classes and the outsiders as the middle or poorer classes. While an *economic* hierarchy of inside and outside is intuitively reinforced by the fact that an inside passage costs more than an outside one, the insiders' scheme of class division is, like persistent notions of British national identity, based more on continuity with "an old *tradition.*" And the hierarchy also becomes implicitly one of authenticity vis-à-vis national origin when it is cast metaphorically as the opposition between the inside passengers, "a porcelain variety of the human race," and "the three miserable delf-ware outsides." While the economic axis of the distinction is inherent again here in the fact that porcelain is more expensive than delf, a division along the lines of national origin is also implied by the fact that porcelain is authentic China originating in the Orient, whereas delf-ware is European "counterfeit China."[9]

The essay is pervaded by such conflicts between authentic national identity on one hand and threatening challenges from an outsider on the other. There is, for instance, a fierce and competitive nationalism informing the central image of the English mail-coach, which becomes a metonymic stand-in for England at large. Carters who block the mail-coach's path "interrupt the great respirations, ebb and flood, *systole* and *diastole,* of the national intercourse" and deserve to be executed at the block as traitors (*CW,* 13:280). De Quincey recalls a dispute with a fellow mail-coach passenger in which he himself argued that it would constitute a challenge to the very authority of England for a Birmingham commercial coach to beat the English mail-coach in a race: "'*Race* us, if you like,' I replied, 'though even *that* has an air of sedition; but not *beat* us. This would have been treason'" (*CW,* 13:282). Despite the fact that both the commercial coach and the mail-coach are English, the competition between them is figured as one between England and an enemy, and opposition to the mail-coach is a seditious challenge to the English state. The mail-coach rather than the commercial conveyance embodies the version of Englishness that matters most in De Quincey's system.

De Quincey cites a precedent for punishing the Birmingham coach's alleged treason: he recounts the tale of a sultan in "some far oriental kingdom" who executed a hawk for killing an eagle, its traditional superior and master (*CW,* 13:282–83). Thus an idealized continuity with an *Oriental* tradition is the precedent for the mail-coach's superior claim to authentic *British* identity. A similar paradox undercuts the porcelain/delf metaphor, which characterizes the inside/outside division as a contest of authenticity between the European (Dutch delf-ware) and the Oriental (Chinese porcelain) but places the Oriental term on top of the hierarchy, implicitly granting authenticity to Chinese rather than European origins. This subtly suggested Oriental basis of the hierarchy becomes more insistent as De Quincey describes the interaction between inside and outside passengers at a stop: "What words, then, could express the horror, and the sense of treason, in that case, which *had* happened, where all three outsides (the trinity of Pariahs) made a vain attempt to sit down at the same breakfast-table or dinner-table with the consecrated four?" (*CW,* 13:274–75). The "consecrated" insiders now stand in opposition to the outside "pariahs"— an unusual word at the time of the essay's composition and still unfamiliar enough nearly half a century later for De Quincey's definitive editor to gloss it as being derived "from the name of the lowest of the Hindoo ranks" (*CW,* 13:274 n). Thus the hierarchy that was previously cast in terms of the Oriental high and European low of China and delf-ware now takes the exclusively Oriental form of the Hindu caste system. The new metaphor does take Europe out of the low position, but it does so only at the price of taking Europe out of the picture altogether, thus giving the Oriental paradigm unchallenged local authority in organizing the inside/outside hierarchy.

I specify local authority because one might argue that the hierarchy is still governed at a more comprehensive level by the spatial division (inside/outside) of the English mail-coach. But even that supposedly quintessential English entity is persistently associated with Oriental paradigms. The Oriental infrastructure is apparent not only in the precedent of the sultan and the hawk but also in the form of the innkeepers' particular placation of the outraged insiders: "if an Indian screen could be found ample enough to plant [the outsiders] out from the very eyes of this high table, or *dais,* it then became possible to assume as a fiction of law that the three delf fellows, after all, were not present" (*CW,* 13:274). The division previously buttressed by the *English* mail-coach is now mediated by the *Oriental* Indian screen. The English and Oriental systems of spatial differentiation perform the same function with equal effectiveness and are readily interchangeable.

De Quincey and his fellow outside passengers—Oxford students who rode the mail-coaches to and from university at holidays—reject the insiders' "bye-laws" of separation as being "of a nature to rouse our scorn," a scorn that seems to hinge on those bye-laws' disregard of the all-important continuity with tradition that is essential to the definition of identity. For, although De Quincey characterizes the insiders' bye-laws as grounded in "an old tradition of public carriages," it is significantly a tradition "derived from the reign of Charles II," a period during which Parliament instituted a number of new privileges for the aristocracy whose traditional ones had been abbreviated by the execution of Charles I. De Quincey snidely alludes to Parliament's legislative manufacture of a spurious class identity with his stab at the insiders' snobbish isolationism: "perhaps, it would have required an act of Parliament," he says, "to restore . . . purity of blood" were an insider to touch an outsider. A similar inference might be drawn from the form of consolation the insiders derive from the separation provided by the Indian screen: "it then became possible to assume *as a fiction of law* that the three delf fellows, after all, were not present" (my emphasis).

From this scorn, "the transition was not very long to systematic mutiny," which is enacted by De Quincey and his fellow outside passengers as a "revolution . . . in the constitution of mail-coach society" (*CW,* 13:273, 277). The revolution consists of reconceiving the position of privilege and authority as the outside instead of the inside of the coach. As an alternative to the discontinuous and speciously instituted "tradition" upon which the insiders base their sense of identity, "revolution" seems at best an ironic choice, for it is by definition an interruption of continuity. But De Quincey argues nonetheless that his particular revolution is continuous with a tradition, and again an Oriental one: "The very same idea [that the box was the superior position] had not long before struck the celestial intellect of China." He relates that, when the English Macartney embassy gave a state-coach to the emperor of China in 1795, the Chinese "resolved by acclamation that the box was the imperial throne, and, for the scoundrel who drove,—he might sit where he could find a perch" (*CW,* 13:275–76). De Quincey and his cronies embrace this comical inversion as an authoritative precedent, and their "revolution . . . in the constitution of mail-coach society" is no less than "a revolution of this same Chinese character" (*CW,* 13:277).

A revolution of a Chinese character would have been densely packed with particular historical significance in De Quincey's era. China was in many ways a good role model for the up-and-coming British Empire: it had preserved its territories for centuries and was internally stable enough to have remained apparently unchanged in its social structure and traditions during that time.[10] For a nascent British empire seeking to cement its authority at home and expand its base abroad, China was an ideal to aspire toward. But English relations with China during De Quincey's lifetime were strained at best. As the East India Company's trading and governmental power in India grew throughout the eighteenth century, China became a crucial market for the unloading of Bengalese opium over which the Company had a monopoly, for the Indo-Chinese trade not only balanced a sizable British trade deficit with China but also yielded a huge profit. The Chinese government, however, severely limited trade with the West and expressly forbade the import of opium. The East India Company responded by secretly assembling a complex smuggling network while publicly trying to negotiate an official arrangement. The Macartney embassy that presented the confusing coach to the Chinese emperor was sent to Peking in 1795 specifically to try to improve trade relations. But controversy ensued when the Chinese imperial government demanded what it had consistently demanded of all previous Western delegations: participation in a masque known as the *kotou,* in which the visitors would portray barbarians crawling on their bellies to seek light from the Lord of the World, who would be played by the Chinese emperor. The choices in the situation were clear and uncomfortable: the British ambassadors could either symbolically acknowledge the Chinese empire as superior to Britain and literally prostrate themselves before it, or they could refuse to participate in the *kotou* and assure the failure of their diplomatic mission.

Obeisance to the Celestial Empire would not necessarily have been out of the question, at least on a symbolic level, for China represented much that Britons of De Quincey's temperament could revere and hope to emulate. But what made China admirable made it frightening as well: China's apparent stability was inspirational, but as a stable imperial power in the regions into which Britain wanted to expand, China was also a threat as a rival empire. The idea of a Chinese-style revolution in English mail-coach society, then, would be at once encouraging and terrifying: while imitation of Chinese precedents might increase English potential for the kind of imperial expansion De Quincey elsewhere offers as the best means of buttressing his vision of a British social structure (about which more in a moment), such imitation would also entail altering—specifically rebuilding in a Chinese image—the society to which that envisioned new order would be expected to pertain, thus potentially nullifying the new order even as it is brought into being. Ultimately such voluntary subjugation to a Chinese precedent would accomplish the opposite of expanding Britain's territorial base in the East by instead rendering England in effect a cultural colony of China.

By choosing to foreground an Oriental precedent for revolution, De Quincey obscures a perhaps more obvious one, the French Revolution, a precedent at least as threatening as the Chinese one, if not more so. For to argue continuity with France would threaten to undo the supposed solidification of British identity brought about in the early part of the nineteenth century when the British identity was most pointedly contrasted to the French one.[11] The French Revolution is nonetheless in many ways at least as accurate a pattern for the mail-coach revolution as the Chinese one, for while the coach-based Chinese revolution maps the English version spatially, the French pattern outlines it socially as the overthrow of an aristocratic ruling class by a traditionally lower class. In the case of De Quincey and many of his fellow Oxonians, the lower class in revolt would be more accurately specified as a middle class, the up-and-coming sons of merchants and industrialists (De Quincey's father was a linen merchant) recently empowered by the opportunity of an Oxford education. It is this Oxford affiliation that gives the outsiders a claim to superiority in De Quincey's value system: contrary to the insiders' view, the outside-riding Oxford men see themselves as in fact "the *élite* of their own generation" (*CW,* 13:273).

One can thus see that, although he revolts against the insiders' version of class hierarchy, De Quincey is far from rejecting the notion of class hierarchy per se. He instead merely corrects the ostensible error of the inside passengers in arrogating to themselves the status that in his opinion belongs to the outside-riding students of Oxford. Even the spatial metaphor with which he structures the new hierarchy smacks of merely another form of class elitism: the Oxonians view the coach-box as "the drawing-room," the proper domain of "gentlemen," and the inside of the coach as "the coal-cellar," implicitly home to stove-tending servants and delivery people (*CW,* 13:275). Key to this revolution, then, is the appropriation of spaces not recognized by the present ruling class as valuable paths to power. The mail-coach, "itself a spiritualised and glorified object to an impassioned heart" (*CW,* 13:272), serves as a patriotic synecdoche for Britain at large. Thus the coach-box, the post from which the glorious machine is controlled, is the logical territory for the ruling class to occupy. The class presently in power is oblivious to this fact, and that obliviousness constitutes the entrée for De Quincey's new ruling-class-to-be.

By extension, the scenario suggests that De Quincey sees global territorial expansion as a means of garnering power for the up-and-coming middle classes: he implies that they might secure their cultural and political authority by assimilating previously undervalued territories (by setting up trading ventures there, the middle classes' forte) and establishing them as both middle-class bastions and crucial positions of power in the nascent British Empire. Thus De Quincey's "Mail-Coach" essay does what Daniel Bivona argues Disraeli's trilogy of novels (also written in the 1840s) does: it "promotes the expansion of England as the inevitable extension of the project of finding a place for the middle and working classes in the governing structure of the country."[12] De Quincey's version, however, envisions not merely *a* place for the middle classes in the governing structure, but *the* place of authority.

Coachmen, Calendars, and Crocodiles

The implicit expansionist logic behind the appropriation of the coach-box becomes more explicit with De Quincey's wry description of his strategy as he descends at a stop, leaving his cloak behind on the box

(*CW,* 13:305)

> *in imitation of a nautical discoverer, who leaves a bit of bunting on the shore of his discovery, by way of warning off the ground the whole human race, and notifying the Christian and heathen worlds, with his best compliments, that he has hoisted his pocket-handkerchief once and for ever upon that virgin soil: thenceforward claiming the* jus dominii *to the top of the atmosphere above it,*

and also the right of driving shafts to the centre of the earth below it; so that all people found after this warning . . . will be treated as trespassers—kicked, that is to say, or decapitated, as circumstances may suggest, by their very faithful servant, the owner of the said pocket-handkerchief.

Cast in the role of the nautical discoverer staking out new terrain to be appropriated and defended against trespassers, De Quincey and his fellow middle-class Oxonians prefigure in "say 1804, or 1805" their own global-scale expansionist projects of the coming decades even as they echo the colonial activities of their merchant forebears.

The salient forms of national expansion being echoed are of course the manifold commercial and governmental operations of the British East India Company.[13] In an essay written during the first opium war, De Quincey invokes the East India Company's precedent, arguing that Britons should systematically assimilate territory in China as the Company had done throughout the previous century in India. Taking to task an assertion in "a London journal of vast authority" that " 'our sole connection with the *Celestial Empire* is mercantile; and in no other point of view need we care one farthing for China, or China for us,' " De Quincey points out that

> *ninety years ago our sole connection with India was mercantile. Army we had none, beyond a few files of musketeers for oriental pomp, and otherwise requisite as a local police. Territory we had none, beyond what was needed for our cows, pigs, and a cabbage garden. Nor had we any scheme for territorial aggrandizement in those days, beyond what was strictly necessary as a means of playing into our commercial measures. . . . What was it that changed that scene? A quarrel with a native prince.*[14]

De Quincey naturalizes British mercantile interests as part of the default scene in India: to have only as much territory as "was strictly necessary as a means of playing into our commercial measures" is to have "none"—the territory necessary for British commercial interests does not count for De Quincey as part of "any scheme for territorial aggrandizement." What does count is the territory acquired after something "changed that scene," and that something is the resistance of someone already in the territory and ruling it, a "native prince."

But although the presence of the disputations native prince is De Quincey's rationale for British schemes of territorial aggrandizement, those schemes themselves fade into invisible background as the "quarrel" becomes a matter not of British aggression but of self-defense against the supposedly despotic prince: "It happens too often in such countries—that to murder is the one sole safeguard against being murdered; insurrection the remedy beforehand against monstrous oppression; and not to be crushed by the wheels of the tiger-hearted despot, you must leap into his chariot, and seize the reins yourself." [15] Using the metaphor of nation-as-coach that he would recycle eight years later in "The English Mail-Coach," De Quincey likens control of the social order in India to control of the reins of a chariot, asserting that to take over the driver's seat is justified as an act of self-defense.

This Indian scenario is mirrored in the revolutionary appropriation of the coach-box in "The English Mail-Coach." There, as we have seen, the driver's seat of the carriage is also figured as the position from which the national entity is controlled, and like the Anglo-Indian merchants, De Quincey takes possession of the driver's seat as a territory to be defended against trespassers. Also like the English merchants who hijack the chariot of India, what the young De Quincey fails at first to realize (or at least fails to acknowledge) is that there is already someone occupying and ruling that territory, or driving that coach. His perception is heightened, however, by a dose of opium:

> *Having mounted the box, I took a small quantity of laudanum. . . . In the taking of laudanum there was nothing extraordinary. But by accident, it drew upon me the special attention of my assessor on the box, the coachman. And in that also there was nothing extraordinary. But by accident, and with great delight, it drew my own attention to the fact that this coachman was a monster in point of bulk, and he had but one eye. . . . Had he been one of the Calendars*
(CW, 13:306) *in the* Arabian Nights, *and had he put down his eye as the price of his criminal curiosity, what right had I to exult in his misfortune? But these personal distinctions . . . identified in an instant an old friend of mine whom I had known in the south for some years as the most masterly of mail-coachmen. He was the man in all Europe that could (if any could) have driven six-in-hand full gallop over* Al-Sirat—*that dreadful bridge of Mahomet, with no side battlements, and of extra room not enough for a razor's edge—leading right across the bottomless gulf.*

Just as the Anglo-Indian merchants tangled with the native "tiger-hearted despot" at the reins, so De Quincey finds himself up against a formidable, implicitly Oriental driver: the mail-coachman is like a Calendar straight out of the *Arabian Nights,* and his control of the reins is measured against an Oriental standard: he could skillfully negotiate "*Al-Sirat*—that dreadful bridge of Mahomet."

And as the rivalry between the East India Company and the Indian princes increased with the English co-optation of Indian commodities, of which opium was the most profitable, so is opium associated with De Quincey's increasing sense of rivalry on the coach-box as the drug leads its young user to perceive for the first time the very presence of his rival and vice versa. The laudanum reveals not only that there is another inhabitant already on the supposedly "virgin soil" (*CW,* 13:305) but also that this rival is unquestionably in control of the territory as "the most masterly of mail-coachmen." The quasi-Oriental Calendar-coachman hearkens back to his professional brother who appeared earlier in the essay, another mail-coachman who "too much resembled a crocodile" (*CW,* 13:286). And the crocodile of course echoes the horrific Orient of the opium dreams described in the *Confessions,* where De Quincey says that "the cursed crocodile became to me the object of more horror than almost all the rest" of the strange Oriental beasts who stalk him, concentrating the accumulated horror of the Orient in a single disease-infested reptile who plagues him with "cancerous kisses" (109–10).

In a sarcastic genealogy of the relationship between humans and crocodiles elaborated in the "Mail-Coach," De Quincey in effect diffuses the crocodile's dominance as he echoes the "revolution in mail-coach society" by merely inverting the hierarchy. He associates the animal at once with an ancient, changeless Orient and a coach to be ridden by the British, thus putting him on the bottommost rung of a British/Oriental hierarchy:

> *Crocodiles, you will say, are stationary. Mr. Waterton tells me that the crocodile does not change,—that a cayman, in fact, or an alligator, is just as good for riding upon as he was in the time of the Pharaohs. That may be; but the reason is that the crocodile does not live fast—he is a slow coach. I believe it is generally understood among naturalists that the crocodile is a blockhead. It is my own impression that the Pharaohs were also blockheads. Now, as the Pharaohs and the crocodile domineered over Egyptian society, this accounts for a singular mistake that prevailed through innumerable generations on the Nile. The crocodile*
>
> (*CW,* 13:288)   *made the ridiculous blunder of supposing man to be meant chiefly for his own eating. Man, taking a different view of the subject, naturally met that mistake by another: he viewed the crocodile as a thing sometimes to worship, but always to run away from. And this continued till Mr. Waterton changed the relations between the animals. The mode of escaping from the reptile he showed to be not by running away, but by leaping on its back booted and spurred. The two animals had misunderstood each other. The use of the crocodile has now been cleared up—viz. to be ridden; and the final aim of man is that he may improve the health of the crocodile by riding him a-foxhunting before breakfast.*

In this, another metaphor for "territorial aggrandizement," backward Orientals and crocodiles both are set straight by the booted and spurred Englishman who effortlessly takes the reins and subjugates the animal to his physical and cultural dominance "by riding him a-foxhunting," thus putting the English once again in the driver's seat and subsuming Oriental form to English tradition.

But like the young opium eater's transient rule of the coach-box, the British dominance implied in this facetious aside about crocodile riding also dissolves when immersed in laudanum. For just as the masterly Calendar-coachman assumed intimidating dimensions after a dose of opium, so does his colleague the crocodile-coachman take frightening control in an opium dream into which "comes a venerable crocodile, in a royal livery of scarlet and gold, or in a coat with sixteen capes [the traditional dress of the mail-coach guard and coachman respectively]; and the crocodile is driving four-in-hand from the box of the Bath mail. And suddenly we upon the mail are pulled up by a mighty dial, sculptured with the hours, and with the dreadful legend of TOO LATE" (*CW,* 13:290 n). Opium shows the quasi-Oriental coachman once again to be driving,[16] a nightmare situation in which the helpless passengers find that it is emphatically "TOO LATE" for something. The graven legend seems to be a reply to the attempted reversal of dominance implied in De Quincey's irreverent ge-nealogy of the crocodile and the Pharaohs. That is, the dream suggests that it is always already too late to alter historical relationships with the Orient-crocodile, for the animal, the region, the culture, are uniquely beyond the reach of historical processes: as De Quincey says, "the crocodile does *not* change," while "all things else undeniably *do*" (*CW,* 13:288–89). This contrast of change and changelessness belies the humiliating reversal the spurred Englishman brings about. Whether on the top or the bottom, in other words, the crocodile-coachman (or the Calendar-coachman) always has been and always will be the driver. De Quincey even hints in a footnote that the crocodile will have the last laugh on his rider, as he compares Waterton's ride to yet another Oriental prece-dent: "The crocodile jibbed and tried to kick, but vainly. He was no more able to throw the squire than Sinbad was to throw the old scoundrel who used his back without paying for it, until he discovered a mode . . . of murdering the old fraudulent jockey, and so circuitously of unhorsing him" (*CW,* 13:288). The "fraudulent" English jockey may be in the saddle for the moment, but he will inevitably be jostled loose and, in accordance with the crocodile's supposition that "man [is] meant chiefly for his own eating," the English rider will presum-ably be ingested and assimilated to his hungry Oriental conveyance—the situa-tion he has always been in anyway, though he has not always been aware of it.[17]

Little England and the Cradle of the Human Race

As the Oriental is revealed to be the precedent for a number of institutions that presumably ground British identity, so does it emerge as an integral element in the foundation of De Quincey's individual identity. It has a place in his own family tree: "I, as well as Pliny," he says in an 1839 essay, "had an uncle, an East Indian uncle." This uncle (his mother's brother, Thomas Penson, after whom De Quincey himself was named), "is 'rather yellow, rather yellow'" and "he is universally a man of princely aspirations and habits. He is not always so Orientally rich as he is reputed; but he is always Orientally munificent" (*CW*, 7:22). Uncle Thomas also appears in the 1856 revision of the *Confessions* as a "bronzed Bengal uncle" who is like "a Bengal tiger," and "whose Indian munificence ran riot upon all occasions" (*CW*, 3:311–13).

When De Quincey calls this uncle "a military man of the Bengal establishment," he means that his Uncle Thomas was an officer in the Military Service of the East India Company in Bengal, and that his income consequently originated in the profits from Oriental commodities—especially opium, which was the chief commercial interest of the Company in Bengal. Thus when De Quincey accepted his uncle's money to finance his own rebellious boondoggle in Wales as an adolescent, he became indirectly implicated in the colonial commerce with the Orient in general and the Indo-Chinese opium trade in particular. But such implication would perhaps have met with young De Quincey's approval, for even at this youthful period he was a staunch advocate of British colonial rule of India, defending the idea against even his uncle's reservations.[18] Furthermore, his initial flight from school had already been financed by a loan of money he knew to have originated in profits from Bengalese opium.[19] Thus De Quincey's genetic inheritance from his "Oriental" uncle is compounded by material bequests with Oriental lineages.

Although De Quincey does mention that his uncle was "a military man of the Bengal establishment, who had come to England on a three-years' leave of absence" (*CW*, 3:311), opening the possibility that his Orientalness was acquired during his tour of duty, he otherwise presents his uncle's Oriental nature as fundamental and seemingly independent of any contact with the Orient. He describes him not, for instance, as "an uncle who had been in India" but instead as "an Indian uncle," a "bronzed Bengal uncle" like "a Bengal tiger," whose Orientalness is inscribed upon his "rather yellow" body. And such an Indian uncle is unexceptional in English families in general: "doubtless you have such an uncle," says De Quincey to his reader, "everybody has an Indian uncle" (*CW*, 7:22). Once again, a deep-rooted English institution turns out to be Oriental at bottom.

De Quincey's sense of this changeless, permanent Orient underlying British institutions is subtle and unexceptionable until it is further uncovered by opium. But then the terror of this deeper excavation informs the torturous

Oriental opium dreams at the heart of the *Confessions of an English Opium-Eater.*
Outlining there "the cause of [his] horror," De Quincey explains that

(108–9)

> *as the cradle of the human race, [Southern Asia] would alone have a dim and
> reverential feeling connected with it. But there are other reasons. . . . The mere
> antiquity of Asiatic things, of their institutions, histories, modes of faith, &c. is
> so impressive, that to me the vast age of the race and name overpowers the sense
> of youth in the individual. A young Chinese seems to me an antediluvian man
> renewed. Even Englishmen, though not bred in any knowledge of such institu-
> tions, cannot but shudder at the mystic sublimity of castes that have flowed
> apart, and refused to mix, through such immemorial tracts of time. . . . The
> vast empires also, into which the enormous population of Asia has always been
> cast, give a further sublimity to the feelings associated with all Oriental names
> or images.*

In addition to being intimidatingly ancient and permanent, according to De
Quincey, the Orient is no less than "the cradle of the human race." The castes
that flowed out of the Orient, then, necessarily would have been the ancestors
of all Europeans, including the passengers on the English mail-coach. Thus, in
the course of attempting to explain the ancient and unbridgeable separateness of
English and Oriental, De Quincey instead backhandedly illustrates the opposite.
"The barrier of utter abhorrence," much like the coach passengers' illusive Indian screen, is finally not a barrier at all. What lies on one side of it is the same
as what lies on the other: both are fundamentally Oriental.

The chief difference between De Quincey's England and his Orient is that
the Orient has maintained its ancient "institutions, histories, modes of faith,
&c." while England has changed. Whereas a progressivist ideology would cast
this change as a positive evolution, De Quincey instead interprets it as a process
of decay. For the contrast between English change and Oriental stasis merely
exposes to him the evanescence of English identity: England is ever-changing
while "the crocodile does *not* change." Stasis in this case means power and authenticity, for the very age and permanence of the monolithic Oriental parent
culture give it an overwhelming authority over its transitory offspring cultures,
an authority that even overrides their individual identities, as "the mere antiquity of Asiatic things, . . . the vast age of the race and name overpowers the
sense of youth in the individual."

The political dimensions of this primeval power come into relief as De
Quincey characterizes the territories into which the ancient Asian castes mi-
grated as "vast empires." The flowing of castes is not merely a random and
diffuse migration but instead a programmatic process of colonization, of imperial expansion not unlike eighteenth- and nineteenth-century British "schemes

of territorial aggrandizement" in the Orient. Like Coleridge and the Higher Critics of the Bible, De Quincey envisions the Orient as the origin of all Western cultures and religions; but instead of seeing this common origin as a positive affirmation of a common culture, he is horrified by the implicit hierarchy arising from it: Western nations and cultures are not proud peers of this time- and space-transcendent Asia but are instead overpowered individuals, subject colonies in its "vast empires."

De Quincey discovers these power relations of origin even within the geological structure of the British Isles. In another essay, he characterizes the terrain of England as merely the detritus of a vast and ancient Asiatic continent: "Even within our domestic limits,—even where little England, in her south-eastern quarter, now devolves so quietly to the sea her own sweet pastoral rivulets— once came roaring down, in pomp of waters, a regal Ganges that drained some hyperbolical continent, some Quinbus Flestrin of Asiatic proportions" (*CW,* 8:10–11). The young and diminutive feminine island of England with "her own sweet pastoral rivulets" is a smaller, quieter, less powerful land than the huge, masculine Quinbus Flestrin (the name the tiny Lilliputians give to Swift's Gulliver), the ancient Asiatic continent with its "pomp of waters, a regal Ganges" that "came roaring down" into England.[20] Thus the pattern we have been tracing—De Quincey's persistent citation of Oriental precedents for English traditions, institutions, and structures—is the symptom of an uneasy worldview in which the Orient is implicitly the precedent not only for all things English but for all things period; and everything descending from the ancient Asiatic continent is less powerful and less permanent than its Oriental parent.[21]

In what was initially intended as a sequel to the *Confessions,* "Suspiria De Profundis" (1845), De Quincey explains that the *Confessions* were meant to illustrate not merely that opium begot fantastic dreams but more importantly that it uncovered and heightened early formative experiences, and that it collaborated with the memories of these experiences to fashion the unusual dream imagery he describes. "Not one agency, but two agencies had co-operated to the tremendous result," he says; "The nursery experience had been the ally and the natural coefficient of the opium" (*CW,* 13:339–40). This prominent role of buried impressions, explains De Quincey, is why the *Confessions* contained so much autobiographical narrative that might have otherwise seemed to the reader to be irrelevant: "because the opium dreams could not always have been understood without a knowledge of these events," he says, "it became necessary to relate them" (*CW,* 13:336).

Anticipating Freud's comparison of the unconscious to a "Mystic Writing-Pad," De Quincey explains the revival of these early impressions in terms of "The Palimpsest of the Human Brain." A palimpsest, he explains, is a sheet of vellum written upon by one generation only to be erased and written upon anew by another. But the "rude chemistry of past ages" that served to clear away the previous writing on the vellum yields to "the more refined chemistry of our own" (*CW*, 13:343), as modern chemicals reveal the ancient writings that subsequent generations thought they had buried beneath their own:

> As the chorus of the Athenian stage unwove through the antistrophe every step
> that had been mystically woven through the strophe, so, by our modern conjura-
> tions of science, secrets of ages remote from each other have been exorcised from
> (CW, 13:345) the accumulated shadows of centuries. Chemistry, a witch as potent as Erictho
> of Lucan . . . has extorted by her torments, from the dust and ashes of forgotten
> centuries, the secrets of a life extinct for the general eye, but still glowing in
> the embers.

The human brain, he explains, similarly retains the early impressions that are written upon it (the "nursery experience"), even if those impressions are, like the original writing on the vellum, "extinct for the general eye." These early impressions become visible again in special circumstances comparable to the application of modern chemistry to the palimpsest: "some merely physical agencies can and do assist the faculty of dreaming almost preternaturally, . . . but beyond all others is opium: which indeed seems to possess a *specific* power in that direction" (*CW*, 13:335). Like the other "modern chemicals" acting on the palimpsest, opium reacts with the opium eater's brain to uncover impressions that are otherwise "extinct for the general eye."

But this model still does not entirely justify the explanatory power De Quincey attributes to such early impressions with respect to the specific content of his opium dreams. Although it is true, for instance, that the story of his endless searching through London crowds for his lost friend Ann helps to explain the repeated appearance of her face in his later dreams, such autobiographical background does little to account for the monumental and timeless Oriental imagery that dominates those dreams—images apparently born of something other than such nursery experience. These Oriental opium dreams hint that the unconscious contains impressions of a deeper order than the ones that arise from individual experience, impressions that apparently even predate the individual. And the metaphors De Quincey uses to theorize about individual consciousness reinforce these hints. He characterizes his version of the unconscious, for instance, in terms of ancient geological strata: "countless are the mysterious handwritings of grief or joy which have inscribed themselves successively upon the palimpsest of your brain", he says; "and, like the annual leaves of aboriginal forests, or the undissolving snows on the Himalaya, or light falling upon light, the endless strata have covered up each other in forgetfulness" (*CW*, 13:348).

Although the metaphor is offered explicitly in relation to memory that encompasses only an individual human life, it nonetheless develops in terms of geological phenomena, progressive layerings in which the contents of each layer are millennia apart in age.

De Quincey's unconscious is thus implicitly structured along an expanded time scale, a dilated dimension he also associates with opium, which has "the extraordinary power . . . (after long use) of amplifying the dimensions of time":

Time it is upon which the exalting and multiplying power of opium spends its operation. Time becomes infinitely elastic, stretching out to such immeasurable and vanishing termini that it seems ridiculous to compute the sense of it, on waking, in expressions commensurate to human life . . . in valuing the virtual time lived during some dreams, the measurement by generations is ridiculous— by millennia is ridiculous; by aeons, I should say, if aeons were more determinate, would be also ridiculous.

(CW, 13:339–40)

De Quincey's unconscious in general, and the one laid bare by opium in particular, has more in common with Jung's model than with Freud's, extending backward into a memory that transcends the individual. Like the palimpsest, he says, his consciousness contains "the dust and ashes of forgotten centuries, the secrets of a life extinct for the general eye, but still glowing in the embers" (CW, 13:348). And opium fans those embers into flames: although the ancient layers usually lie invisible and dormant, "by the searchings of opium, all these can revive in strength" (CW, 13:348). Opium excavates the ancient strata, appearing to "have backed upon each phoenix in the long *regressus,* and forced him to expose his ancestral phoenix, sleeping in the ashes below his own ashes" (CW, 13:346).

After long use of this dream-heightening and time-dilating drug, De Quincey reports, "the whole economy of the dreaming faculty had been convulsed beyond all precedents on record," prompting "a stricter scrutiny of the past" (CW, 131:339–40). But "the past" itself necessarily loses determinate boundaries in the face of this elastic opium time, and the opium eater of "Suspiria" scrutinizes a different nursery experience than the one traced through the early parts of the *Confessions.* This alternative nursery experience is formative enough, encompassing enough, and distant enough to account for the infinite, timeless opium dreams, for chains of events that are not "commensurate to human life." And it accordingly relates to a different cradle than the one in which the opium eater's nanny rocked him: as with the action of modern chemistry on the palimpsest, a dose of laudanum dredges up ancient layers of "Nilotic mud" to enfold the dreamer in their primordial ooze, to rock him once again in the Oriental "cradle of the human race." Just as layers of Oriental detritus form the geological basis of England, so are they the structure of each individual English unconscious. And opium is the modern chemical that restores the original writing on the palimpsest, the archaeological tool, the acid that lays bare the fossil in the rock.

De Quincey offers a model of this nursery experience within "Suspiria" in a scene that is at once literal and metaphorical, addressing the elasticity of the individual consciousness's time in terms of English versus Oriental time. The scene, uncovered in an "exploring voyage of inquest into hidden scenes or forgotten scenes of human life" (*CW,* 13:356), opens with the entrance of a five-year-old English girl who seems at first glance to be a harmonious part of the representative English thicket into which she comes "bounding like a fawn, . . . loving, natural, and wild as any one of her neighbours for some miles round,—namely, leverets, squirrels, and ring-doves." But this vision of harmony proves deceptive, for "what will surprise you most is that, although a child of pure English blood, she speaks very little English, but more Bengalee than perhaps you will find it convenient to construe" (*CW,* 13:358). The reason for this seemingly incongruous hybridity becomes apparent as a quasi-parental Oriental influence emerges in the background:

> *That is her ayah, who comes up from behind at a pace so different from her*
> *youthful mistress's. . . . In reality, the child has passed her whole life in the arms*
> *of this ayah. She remembers nothing other than* her; *eldest of things is the ayah*
> *in her eyes; and if the ayah should insist on her worshipping herself as the goddess*
> *Railroadina or Steamboatina, that made England, and the sea, and Bengal, it*
> *is certain that the little thing would do so, asking no question but this,—whether*
> *kissing would do for worshipping.*

(*CW,* 13:359)[22]

The little girl echoes De Quincey's "little England, in her south-eastern quarter" as she stands in contrast to her wizened ayah, who recalls the ancient Quinbus Flestrin, the Asiatic continent that roared into England aeons ago, before England *was* England. The Oriental ayah moves "at a pace so different from her youthful mistress's," operating on a different, expanded time scale, and is the "eldest of things" in her young English mistress's eyes. The little girl's consciousness thus parallels that of the opium dreamer, standing awestruck in the face of the vast age of the Oriental image before her, an image so impressive that she is even ready to worship it as an originary "goddess . . . that made England."

This scene of nursery experience serves as a kind of parable or allegory: it treats the differential in time structures that De Quincey elsewhere couches in terms of the difference between the day-to-day unconscious and the timeless one opened up by opium, and it associates the inflated time with an ageless, powerful Oriental force while marking the familiar time as characteristic of a small and vulnerable English sensibility. It also overtly attributes to the little girl what has been implicit in De Quincey's responses to the Orient: a tendency to extrapolate from this differential England's origins in the Orient, an idea that leads irresistibly to a sense of a power relation in which the Orient stands in loco parentis, commanding English reverence and submission, even worship.

The young girl's worshipful attitude toward her ayah also significantly mirrors De Quincey's dependence upon opium—or, as he characterizes the malady in the same essay, his "prostration before the dark idol" (*CW,* 13:337). Opium rules the author in a relationship of dominance and submission he describes several times as "the tyranny of opium," and he repeatedly attempts to resist this tyranny. As in the cases of the mail-coach and the chariot of India, "insurrection is the remedy beforehand against monstrous oppression," and the opium eater again mounts a revolution. "At the close of [the *Confessions*]," he says in "Suspiria," "the reader was instructed to believe, and *truly* instructed, that I had mastered the tyranny of opium. The fact is that *twice* I mastered it, and by efforts even more prodigious in the second of these cases than in the first" (*CW,* 13:336). But there is a third conflict with a decidedly different outcome:

(*CW,*
13:336–37)

> *I endeavoured, with some feeling of panic, for a third time to retrace my steps. But I had not reversed my motions for many weeks when I became aware that this was impossible. Or, in the imagery of my dreams, which translated every-thing into their own language, I saw, through vast avenues of gloom, those tower-ing gates of ingress which hitherto had always seemed to stand open now at last barred against my retreat and hung with funeral crape.*

De Quincey emphasizes the fact that he successfully revolted *twice*, recalling, perhaps not coincidentally, the two English insurrections he advocated in India and China. As England emerged victorious from those two international conflicts, so does De Quincey succeed in his. His third attempt, however, not only fails but also preempts any future attempts, assuring his prostration forever. This ultimate failure is inherent in the terms of the illusory triumphs: "twice I sank, and twice I rose again," he says, as the implicit drowning metaphor meanwhile insists that he will sink a third time never to rise again. The moments when De Quincey finds his head above water are the aberrations rather than the norm.

The supposedly successful revolts, then, emerge in this context as merely moments of willful blindness. Perhaps also the celebrated British coups in the Orient merely imposed new myths over the top of Oriental origins but never superseded them. Just as medieval monks erased classical texts from palimpsests to write new nationalist romances over them, Britons have superimposed a proud tradition of a courageous, dominant British identity atop their Oriental origins. But the British nationalist myths only temporarily mask the ineradicable, primary Oriental character that will always command British reverence. Britons may write over the palimpsest with a new text, suggests De Quincey, but they never really succeed in erasing the original one, which remains and reemerges from time to time (especially in the presence of opium), just as the palimpsest's "Grecian tragedy seemed to be displaced, but was *not* displaced, by the monkish legend" (*CW,* 13:348).

As opium digs up the Oriental buried beneath the British, so does the opium eater expose an underground of other opium eaters like himself:

(*CW,*
3:211–12)
> *The whole class of opium-eaters . . . [is] I am sorry to say, a very numerous class indeed. Of this I became convinced, some years ago, by computing, at that time, the number in one small class of English society (the class of men distin- guished for talents, or of eminent station) who were known to me, directly or indirectly, as opium-eaters . . . Now, if one class, comparatively so limited, could furnish so many scores of cases (and that within the knowledge of one single inquirer), it was a natural inference that the entire population of England would produce a proportionable number.*

Informal surveys confirm his suspicions:

(*CW,* 3:212)
> *Three London druggists, in widely remote quarters of London, from whom I happened lately to be purchasing small quantities of opium, assured me that the number of amateur opium-eaters (as I may term them) was, at that time, im- mense . . . This evidence respected London only. But . . . some years ago, on passing through Manchester, I was informed by several cotton manufacturers that their work-people were rapidly getting into the practice of opium-eating; so much so, that on a Saturday afternoon the counters of the druggists were strewed with pills of one, two, three grains, in preparation for the known demand of the evening.*

The community of English opium eaters in De Quincey's profile thus spans every socioeconomic class and relative position of power in British society as well as several geographic regions, forming an overarching "class of opium- eaters."

So, De Quincey suggests, opium has a firm power base in British society, boasting slaves at all levels of privilege and prestige. But this dominion is all but invisible, for it is impossible to recognize the opium slaves hidden like pod people throughout British society. One may even be a slave oneself without knowing it: "under such treacherous disguises [as patent medicines secretly con- taining opium] multitudes are seduced into a dependency which they had not foreseen upon a drug which they had not known; . . . and thus the case is not rare that the chain of abject slavery is first detected when it has inextricably wound itself about the constitutional system" (*CW,* 3:223–24). De Quincey stops just short of the assertion that the entire British population is held in "abject slavery" to opium whether they know it or not. This paranoid fantasy would be closely related to the horror of his opium dreams, which expose Britons as having unwittingly been trumped in their "schemes of territorial aggrandizement"; they have always already been assimilated and dominated by the very peoples and regions they wish to assimilate and dominate. In fact Britain is and always has been those peoples and regions, but a lesser version, a faded derivative, a degraded child that is forever at a disadvantage with its powerful elder. England is the naive little girl who has never been independent of her Oriental mistress ("in reality, the child has passed her whole life in the arms of this ayah"), and she is completely in thrall to the powerful older woman ("if the ayah should insist on her worshipping herself as the goddess . . . that made England, and the sea, and Bengal, it is certain that the little thing would do so").

Pain Is Pleasure

One question looms large over De Quincey's autobiographical prose: why does he continue to use opium when he verifies again and again that it instigates agonizing crises of identity? It is tempting to answer by invoking twentieth-century models of addiction, which emphasize tolerance and withdrawal as factors that encourage continued and increasing use of "addictive" substances,[23] even though those substances produce increasingly unpleasant sensations and may ultimately cease to provide any pleasurable ones. The user persists, as the addiction model would have it, because withdrawal symptoms make the alternative of abstinence too painful to endure. Such a model initially seems promising as an entrée to explaining the case of De Quincey, who continues to take opium despite his sense that it dissolves his very identity. But the addiction model is limited by, among other factors, its implicit presupposition of stable definitions of pleasure and pain. Freud is more sensitive to crossovers and contradictions as he addresses the counterintuitive operation of these conventionally defined poles in motivating compulsive repetitive behavior:

> It is clear that the greater part of what is re-experienced under the compulsion to repeat must cause the ego unpleasure, since it brings to light activities of the repressed instinctual impulses. That, however, is unpleasure of a kind [that] does not contradict the pleasure principle: unpleasure for one system and simultaneously satisfaction for the other. But we come to a new and remarkable fact, namely that the compulsion to repeat also recalls from the past experiences which include no possibility of pleasure, and which can never, even long ago, have brought satisfaction even to instinctual impulses which have since been repressed.[24]

Freud seems to be describing exactly the situation of De Quincey, whose opium use "recalls from the past experiences which include no possibility of pleasure." Freud gets around the seeming impossibility of pleasure in such circumstances by reconsidering conventional conceptions of pleasure: "If we are not to be shaken in our belief in the wish-fulfilling tenor of dreams by the dreams of traumatic-neurotics, . . . we may be driven to reflect on the mysterious masochistic trends of the ego." [25] In other words, dreamers of recurrent and torturous dreams like De Quincey's perhaps blur the boundary between pleasure and pain, or even reverse their conventional positions, taking something much like what would usually be called pleasure from what convention would label as painful.

One could extrapolate from this a form of masochistic repetition compulsion as an explanation of De Quincey's opium use, a process in which the opium eater chronically replays, through the dreams his opium use provides, an imagined original moment of Oriental infection. This repetitive behavior is perhaps an unconscious attempt to gain retroactive control of the disruptive experience and cancel its aftereffects. But the opium dreams, far from bringing De Quincey closer to resolving the traumatic moment, instead force upon him the realization that there is no originary traumatic moment to relive, but rather a beginningless and endless trauma in which every attempt to separate English and Oriental, self and other, only further illustrates how unified they are, always have been, and apparently always will be. De Quincey's repetition compulsion, or his "addiction," then, seems to be masochistically to enact over and over again a self-annihilation. [26]

But to add yet another level of instability—or, dare I say, to *uncover* it— one must at least acknowledge the contradiction inherent in applying *any* model of individual psychology to De Quincey's case, for he is fundamentally concerned with the breakdown of the very idea of the individual. To echo my question in the introduction of this discussion, where does the self end and the other begin? The question was central also to Coleridge's anxieties as he traced the outlines of a collective British body, a body that was not clearly differentiable from his own supposedly individual one. The problem extended to the horizon for Coleridge, as he found that even the collective British body also bleeds into the other large-scale entity of the Orient (and vice versa). But De Quincey takes Coleridge's insights even a step further: he views such non-differentiation not as a breach or an infection of one entity by another but instead as a unity that always has been and always will be in place. [27]

IV

"Accepting a Matter of Opium as a Matter of Fact"

The Moonstone, *Opium, and Hybrid Anglo-Indian Culture*

> *Do we suppose . . . that in the next century, if the colo-*
> *nial . . . connection has been maintained and has become*
> *closer, England itself will not be very much modified and*
> *transformed?*
>
> Sir John
> Seeley, *The*
> *Expansion of*
> *England*

IN CHAPTER 10 of Wilkie Collins's *The Moonstone,* Rachel Verinder appears at her coming-of-age birthday dinner wearing the exotic Indian diamond she has just inherited from her late uncle, Colonel John Herncastle. She and the rest of the company are titillated when one of her guests, the eminent Indian explorer Mr. Murthwaite, warns her that "I know a certain city [in India], and a certain temple in that city, where, dressed as you are now, your life would not be worth five minutes' purchase." Rachel's response is typical of eighteenth- and nineteenth-century Britons faced with representations of an exotic and potentially threatening—but very importantly *distant*—Orient: "Miss Rachel, safe in England, was quite delighted to hear of her danger in India" (101).[1] Rachel's tacit belief in the sheltering power of surrounding English culture and institutions is diametrically opposed, however, to the sentiments of the previous owner of the diamond, her Uncle Herncastle. An anecdote told earlier in the novel by Rachel's cousin and suitor, Franklin Blake, relates that Herncastle once asked Franklin's father to assume responsibility for the security of the gem, for the colonel claimed that "neither he nor his precious jewel was safe in any house, in any quarter of the globe, which they occupied together" (68). The elder Mr. Blake, sharing Rachel's faith in protective English institutions, scoffed at the colonel's fears: "As for the danger of his being murdered, and the precautions devised to preserve his life and his piece of crystal, this was the nineteenth century, and any man in his senses had only to apply to the police." But although Mr. Blake's first impulse was to dismiss Herncastle's misgivings as the ramblings of a man who "had been a notorious opium-eater for years past," he needed access to some important documents in the colonel's possession, and "if the only way of getting at the valuable papers . . . was by accepting a matter of opium as a matter of fact," says Franklin, "my father was quite willing" (69).

The ironic twist here is that the novel ultimately proves the elder Mr. Blake to have been quite right to accept Herncastle's story as fact, albeit for the wrong reasons, for the colonel's seemingly outlandish paranoia was in fact justified: he did live under a constant threat, specifically from three mysterious Hindu Brahmins who followed the diamond from India and were expected to stop at nothing to retrieve it. For the same reasons, Rachel Verinder is not, as she supposes, safe amidst the sheltering institutions of England enjoying the thrill of a danger that exists only in the benignly distant Orient of her imagination, for it later comes to light that the very hazard Mr. Murthwaite described as operative in India was at that very moment looming literally in her own backyard in the shape of the three murderously determined Brahmins keeping a vigil at the rear patio. In short, *The Moonstone* ultimately illustrates that Colonel Herncastle's matter of opium *is* a matter of fact, for the novel makes it clear in this and other instances that dangerous Indian threats, though not always evident, are suffused throughout England and English culture and might surface at any moment with dire consequences. But these dangerous Indian threats might be characterized with equal accuracy as seductive Indian thrills, for Britons often actively court the same alien elements that they view at other moments with fear and loathing, and it is this paradox that accounts for much of the tension surrounding the Moonstone and other traces of India in the putatively English culture of the novel. The exposure of this tension, like the ultimate solution of the novel's mystery, is enabled by what Collins portrays as the mysterious power of opium, which is itself linked in midcentury English culture with India in ways that are similarly both thrilling and threatening.

"The Brightest Jewel in the British Crown"

Although opium plays a crucial role with respect to the development of the central paradoxes in the novel, the ambivalent object that Collins most deliberately links with India is the eponymous Moonstone, which he endows with idiosyncrasies that significantly parallel the contemporary English popular consciousness of India.[2] As the object of centuries of ownership disputes between Hindus and Moslems, for instance, the Moonstone echoes the authoritative English version of the history of India—and Collins's chief source for historical background to his narrative—J. Talboys Wheeler's *The History of India*. Wheeler divides Indian history into, first, a Hindu period he calls "the Vedic and Brahmanic Ages" and, second, a "Period of Mussulman Rule," both of which serve as prelude to an implicitly teleological epoch, "the rise of British ascendancy."[3] This asymmetrical structure also characterizes the history of the Moonstone, whose transfer from Hindu to Moslem hands is finally only background to its British sojourn. The Moonstone's genealogy comes at the beginning of the novel as part of a prologue that ultimately explains how the Indian gem fell into British hands at the Siege of Seringapatam (1799), a choice of setting that itself underscores further parallels between the diamond and its national counterpart. The Siege of Seringapatam concluded a series of conflicts between the East India Company and the infamous "Tiger of Mysore," Tipu Sultan, who had constituted the most serious threat to the Company's hegemony since he began mounting attempts in 1790 to recover territories the Company had claimed as its own. Although he appeared to have been decisively defeated in 1792 (the Third Anglo-Mysore War), he was preparing to march again by 1798, this time under the aegis of an alliance with France. Governor-General Richard Colley Wellesley responded by sending Company forces to Tipu's capital of Seringapatam (the Fourth Anglo-Mysore War), where they defeated the Mysore army and killed the sultan himself after a siege lasting nearly a month. The British victory was sealed by a peace treaty that granted Wellesley the prerogative of unlimited intervention in the internal affairs of Mysore and thus, as Wellesley himself put it, "utterly annihilated the spirit of insubordination and contempt which for some time past has been gaining ground among the Mohammedan subjects."[4] The Siege of Seringapatam played a pivotal role in Anglo-Indian history, then, as it enabled Britons more complacently to regard India as a British possession. Thus the parallel with the Moonstone: just as the Siege of Seringapatam put India more securely into collective British hands, so in Collins's novel does it put the Moonstone into the individual British hands of the young Colonel John Herncastle, who is so obsessed with the diamond that he risks his own life and commits murder amidst the chaos of the battle in Tipu's palace so that he may steal it from the sultan's vaults.

The powerful appeal of the exotic Indian diamond is a peculiarly appropriate choice of metonym for the obsessive English fascination with India, for the historical playing out of that attraction was also mediated largely through Indian gems. Tipu's jewelry, for instance, assumed an irresistible allure similar to that of the Moonstone for his English conquerors, and the intensity of this attraction, like that of Herncastle's obsession with the Moonstone, is not readily explainable merely in terms of exchange value.[5] As one firsthand account has it, the soldier who ultimately killed Tipu seemed, like Herncastle, more interested in getting his hands on the sultan's finery than protecting his own life as he "seized the Sultaun's sword-belt, which was very rich, and attempted to pull it off" while Tipu "made a cut at the soldier . . . and wounded him about the knee."[6] Another similar instance presents an even more pointed disjunction between economic value and what we might call "exotic value": Governor-General Wellesley declined the House of Commons's offer of £100,000 as his share of the loot confiscated from Seringapatam, but he eagerly accepted a star and badge made from some of Tipu's jewels.[7] The enigmatic drives on the part of these British individuals to possess Tipu's jewelry mirror the collective terms of a desiring England and a desired India as figured in the contemporary discourse of the nascent British Empire. This was, after all, the era when India was fondly dubbed "the brightest jewel in the British Crown,"[8] a nickname redolent of the splendor of that rich and magical imagined domain, the seductive and mysterious Orient of popular Oriental tales.

It is this intangible exotic other that Tipu's jewelry seems to reify and make available for British possession, and it is what Herncastle brings back to England in the form of the spectacular Indian diamond he has stolen from Tipu's vaults. Once in England, the Moonstone exercises a strange magnetic power over Britons there just as it did at a presumably safe distance in India. The butler, Gabriel Betteredge, describes the delirium of the party at Frizinghall, the Verinders' Yorkshire country manor, when the diamond is first unveiled:

(96)

> There stood Miss Rachel at the table, like a person fascinated, with the Colonel's unlucky Diamond in her hand. There, on either side of her, knelt the two Bouncers [Rachel's cousins], devouring the jewel with their eyes, and screaming with ecstasy every time it flashed on them in a new light. There, at the opposite side of the table, stood Mr. Godfrey, clapping his hands like a large child and singing out softly, "Exquisite! exquisite!"

The Indian diamond hypnotizes and/or infantilizes everyone who looks at it. Even the sharp and cynical Betteredge attests that "when you looked down into the stone, you looked into a yellow deep that drew your eyes into it so that they saw nothing else" (97). There are even sexual overtones to this strange charisma, as the women "[scream] with ecstasy" and Betteredge suggestively admits that "the Diamond laid such a hold on *me* that I burst out with as large an 'O' as the Bouncers themselves" (97).

The thrall in which the Moonstone holds its English admirers suggests that, if the Indian diamond brings home an exciting exoticism, this act of importation also has a dark underside reminiscent of Coleridge's anxieties about Oriental commodities and retributive invasion, an association more than reinforced by the dangerous Indian traces the diamond trails behind it. "Here was our quiet English house," says Betteredge, "suddenly invaded by a devilish Indian Diamond—bringing after it a conspiracy of living rogues" (67). The rogues in question are the infamous trio of Hindu Brahmins who are consistently characterized as predatory and insidious. The novel's expert on Indian culture, Mr. Murthwaite, warns of them that "those men will wait their opportunity with the patience of cats, and will use it with the ferocity of tigers" (108), and he regards their appearance at Frizinghall on the evening of Rachel's birthday as evidence that they have had the opportunistic cunning to "wait till the Diamond was at the disposal of a young girl, who would innocently delight in wearing the magnificent jewel at every possible opportunity" (333–34). When the gem is missing the following morning, the Brahmins are predictably the prime suspects as Franklin Blake speculates that "one of them might have slipped into the hall . . . The fellow may have been under the sofa when my aunt and Rachel were talking about where the Diamond was to be put for the night. He would only have to wait till the house was quiet, and there it would be in the cabinet, to be had for the taking" (117).

The threat that these Brahmins embody is a historically as well as sexually charged one, for the persistent juxtaposition of ferocious Indians and vulnerable Englishwomen running through the suspicions and warnings about them resembles another India-related popular discourse in which Collins himself had twice engaged several years earlier, the spate of English outcries against the Sepoy Mutiny of 1857.[9] Patrick Brantlinger characterizes the genre as consistently reducing to a simplistic binary opposition: "on the one hand are the motiveless, bloodthirsty mutineers and 'the madness of superstition'; on the other, the spotless innocence of English women and children and of 'Christian worship.'"[10] Much of the horror figured by the trope is in response to the apprehension that hostile Indian men can penetrate an English domestic space and take possession of it, a process represented in portrayals of the Mutiny and elsewhere as both a figurative rape of England and a literal rape of English women.[11] It is this scenario that lurks not so far beneath Franklin Blake's speculation about the Hindu under the sofa cunningly watching for the moment when he might sneak into Rachel's bedroom and steal her diamond, an act also implicitly equated with sexual violation.[12]

But despite all the menacing potential they represent, these Indians are all the more threatening and fascinating for the fact that they do not outwardly seem violent. In fact they are, like the Moonstone, hypnotically charming. The butler, Betteredge, himself attests that they have "the most elegant manners," manners that are even, he says, "superior to my own." The crotchety lawyer Matthew Bruff likewise praises the chief Brahmin's "graceful politeness of manner," which again sets him above Englishmen: he was, says Bruff, "the perfect model of a client" (325), and the lawyer prefers the Indian's society to that of the Englishman who visits him immediately afterward and is "in every respect such an inferior creature to the Indian" (327). These captivating Indians know how to exploit the English fascination with a mystified Orient. In addition to their personal magnetism, they twice employ the bait of "an ancient Oriental manuscript, richly illuminated" when they want to search an Englishman for the Moonstone; they leave him alone in a room with the manuscript, then grab him from behind while his "attention [is] absorbed . . . by this beautiful work of Indian art" (239, 242).

"The Mixture of Some Foreign Race in His English Blood"

The almost preternatural force exercised by the Orient over the English imagination is also associated with the character who is the novel's most condensed representative of Anglo-Oriental cultural mixing, the opium-addicted apothecary, Ezra Jennings. This strange man has an inexplicably powerful effect on Franklin Blake, who claims that he "produced too strong an impression on me to be immediately dismissed from my thoughts" (372) at a time when "it seemed perfectly unaccountable . . . that any human being should have produced an impression on me at all!" (373). "Ezra Jennings made some inscrutable claim on my sympathies," he says, "which I found it impossible to resist" (417). Blake attributes this haunting force to Jennings's exotic air of having "the mixture of some foreign race in his English blood" (420), an impression born out by Jennings's own account of himself: "I was born, and partly brought up, in one of our colonies. My father was an Englishman; but my mother—" (420). Although Jennings's cryptic allusions leave the non-English contribution to his own identity unspecified, Franklin Blake is nonetheless quick to fill in the blank with the Orient: "His complexion was of a gipsy darkness, . . . his nose presented the fine shape and modelling so often found among the ancient people of the East, so seldom visible among the newer races of the West" (371).

Despite his strikingly Oriental facial features, however, the equivocality of Jennings's Anglo-Oriental identity is encoded on his body in a number of ways, the most jarring of which is a bizarre conflict between black and white. His hair, as Franklin Blake describes it,

(371)

> had lost its colour in the most startling and capricious manner. Over the top of his head it was still of the deep black which was its natural colour. Round the sides of his head—without the slightest gradation of grey to break the force of the extraordinary contrast—it had turned completely white. The line between the two colors preserved no sort of regularity. At one place, the white hair ran up into the black; at another, the black hair ran down into the white.

Jennings, then, is not a smooth blend of English and Oriental, black and white, but a contested territory permeated by "extraordinary contrast." The contrast is born chiefly of superimposition, for black is the "natural colour" of his hair, whereas white is what it has "turned," punctuated by points of insurgence. Ezra Jennings's startling hair thus serves as a metaphor not only for the mixing of black and white but more pointedly for the *colonization* of black *by* white.

This inscription on Jennings's body of the blending of East and West is reinforced in the De Quinceyan terms of a young England superimposed over an ancient Orient when Franklin Blake speaks of "the puzzling contradiction between his face and figure which made him look old and young together" (417). Jennings himself, however, attributes his premature decrepitude to an "incurable internal complaint," of which he says, "The one effectual palliative in my case, is—opium. To that potent and all-merciful drug, I am indebted for a respite of many years from my sentence of death. But even the virtues of opium have their limit. The progress of the disease has gradually forced me from the use of opium to the abuse of it. I am feeling the penalty at last" (429–30). This lament serves as yet another encrypted index of the blending of East and West—or, more specifically, England and India—for Jennings's "internal complaint" and his recourse to opium echo the ills and palliatives of British India. While the East India Company's Anglo-Indian colonies were suffering from serious internal complaints such as the 1857 Mutiny, they too were kept alive by opium, for the Company's monopoly over the poppy crops in Bengal and its booming illegal opium trade with China were largely responsible for keeping its accounts in the black. But, as in Jennings's case, this boom was a curse as well, for maintenance of the trade with China had necessitated two "opium wars" in midcentury (1839–42 and 1856–60) that were devastatingly expensive both economically and politically. Indeed the rhetoric of critique that arose in response to these wars often sounded much like Ezra Jennings's lament of having progressed "from the use of opium to the abuse of it" and of "feeling the penalty at last." [13]

The side effect of Jennings's opium use that is most important to the development of the novel's plot, the unusual prescience he imbibes with his laudanum, also reinforces his connection with India as it ties him to a tradition of Oriental magic that is pointedly evoked elsewhere in the novel by the three Brahmins' ability to divine the Moonstone's whereabouts from images in a pool of "thick, sweet-smelling liquor, as black as ink" (82). In both of these instances, though, the Oriental magic works only in cooperation with an English catalyst: the Indians' black liquor is apparently useless without the aid of "a little delicate-looking light-haired English boy" (49) who reads its reflections, and Jennings's opium enables him to piece together his fragmentary insights only after he joins forces with the Englishman Franklin Blake. After he questions Blake, the surgeon's assistant is able to make sense of the incoherent ramblings he heard at the bedside of his boss, the fevered surgeon, Mr. Candy, and he pieces together a narrative of the evening of the Moonstone's disappearance: Mr. Candy clandestinely slipped a dose of laudanum into Franklin Blake's brandy and water in order to win an argument concerning the effectiveness of medicine in treating insomnia. The result, as Jennings deduces with the help of Blake's information, was that Blake entered a trancelike state and acted out his anxiety over the stone's safety by taking it from Rachel's room. What he did with it after taking it, though, is beyond Jennings's power to see. It is at this point that the relationship between the half-Oriental surgeon's assistant and the Englishman most strongly resembles the one between the Brahmins and their English boy, as Jennings and Blake similarly must resort to the administration of a mysterious and powerful liquid—in this case a second dose of laudanum—to enable the revelation of hidden information. In case the reading audience is slow of perception, however, Betteredge underscores the parallel with the complaint that "it ends . . . in a conjuring trick being performed on Mr. Franklin Blake, by a doctor's assistant with a bottle of laudanum" (453).

Betteredge's grumblings foreground the anxiety-inducing hierarchy around Jennings and Blake's experiment: it is the compromisedly Oriental Jennings who is in control while the Englishman is in a vulnerable state of altered consciousness. Similar anxieties cluster around the parallel case of the Brahmins' act of divination, which comes to be associated with the by now familiar fears of possible Indian domination of vulnerable English subjects—this time "a little delicate-looking light-haired English boy." Betteredge's daughter, Penelope, and the lodge keeper's daughter have, as Betteredge says, "[taken] it into their heads that the boy was ill-used by the foreigners—for no reason that I could discover except that he was pretty and delicate-looking" (49). Penelope describes the seeing ritual to her father:

(50)

> Well, when the Indian said, "Hold out your hand," the boy shrunk back, and shook his head, and said he didn't like it. The Indian, thereupon, asked him (not at all unkindly), whether he would like to be sent back to London, and left where they had found him, sleeping in an empty basket in a market—a hungry, ragged, and forsaken little boy. This, it seems, ended the difficulty. The little chap unwillingly held out his hand. Upon that, the Indian—first touching the boy's head, and making signs over it in the air—then said, "Look." The boy became quite stiff, and stood like a statue, looking into the ink in the hollow of his hand.

Betteredge discounts the young women's fears that the boy is being mistreated, and his skepticism presumably arises from the implication that, far from making the boy's lot worse, the Brahmins have saved him from a life of starvation in the mean streets of London. But what lulls Betteredge is precisely what agitates his daughter: this relationship of patronage between the English boy and his Indian benefactors ironically reverses the putative one between England and India along the lines of De Quincey's little Bengalee-speaking English girl's prostration before her ancient ayah. It is thus easy to see Penelope and the lodge keeper's daughter as reacting to an anxiety much like the one Franklin Blake manifests when he imagines the Indian beneath the couch: the fear that Indian men can penetrate the English domestic space and reverse the power dynamics of Empire, exercising a potentially retributive dominion over vulnerable and innocent English women and children in their English homes.

It is an important difference between the two parallel scenarios of Jennings and Blake and the Brahmins and their boy, however, that one involves parties of starkly differentiated races and nationalities (the Indians and the English boy), whereas the other takes shape around overtly hybrid individuals. Ezra Jennings's hybridity is emphasized by his jarring appearance, but Franklin Blake's national character, though less overtly fragmented, is arguably even less coherent. Although Blake is English by birth, his Englishness is compromised by what Betteredge calls "the puzzling shifts and transformations in Mr. Franklin [which] were due to the effect upon him of his foreign training." He explains:

(76–77)

> *At the age when we are all of us most apt to take our colouring, in the form of a reflection from the colouring of other people, he had been sent abroad, and had been passed on from one nation to another, before there was time for any colouring more than another to settle itself on him firmly. As a consequence of this, he had come back with so many different sides to his character, all more or less jarring with each other, that he seemed to pass his life in a state of perpetual contradiction with himself. . . . He had his French side, and his German side, and his Italian side—the original English foundation showing through, every now and then, as much as to say "Here I am, sorely transmogrified, as you see, but there's something of me left at the bottom of him still."*

There are of course key differences between the hybrid personalities of Blake and Jennings: one appears to be composed entirely of European components while the other is Anglo-Oriental; one is apparent only through contrasts of different nationally coded behaviors while the other is overtly visible in juxtapositions of black and white on the body; one is acquired socially while the other is ostensibly inherited genetically. Their side-by-side presentation, however, suggests that a hybrid nature can be generated as forcefully through a sort of contaminative contact as through putative genetic encoding.

The precedent set by Blake's acquired hybridity, his personality-altering "[passing] from one nation to another," has resonant implications later in the novel with respect to the mixing of English and Oriental. Blake recounts that, after being disappointed in his romance with Rachel Verinder, he went "wandering in the East" (339) in order to "force his attention away from the exclusive contemplation of his own sorrow" and cause "the pang of remembrance [to lose] its worst bitterness" (340)—in other words, he uses the Orient as an anodyne not unlike opium to deaden pain and alter his consciousness. And his consciousness is indeed altered when he returns from his Eastern wanderings, as the results of the second dose of laudanum illustrate. Jennings cites it as a prerequisite to the success of his experiment that Franklin Blake be "as nearly as possible, in the same position, physically and morally, in which the opium found [him] last year" (439). But the at best limited success of the experiment suggests that this precondition has not been met, for although the second dose of laudanum causes Blake to duplicate his previous actions up to the point of taking the diamond, he passes out immediately afterward. Jennings anticipated the possibility of such a failure and attributed it in advance to the obvious difficulty of recreating the environment and stimuli of a year before. But it is surely at least as significant that Blake has spent part of the intervening year immersed in the Orient, where his extraordinarily absorbent personality has soaked up a dose of Eastern influence, critically altering the "position, physically and morally" in which the second dose of laudanum finds him. The difference between Blake and Jennings is thus ultimately more a matter of degree than of kind, for Blake too bears traces of Anglo-Oriental hybridity.

This pervasive and disquieting hybridity is, as we have seen, highlighted by the character of Ezra Jennings, and it is perhaps because of this highlighting function that the apothecary is regarded as a pariah by his adopted English community. As Betteredge says, "right or wrong, we none of us liked him or trusted him" (187), chiefly because "his appearance is against him, to begin with" (372), an appearance that is most impressive for its contrasts with *itself* rather than its differences from the appearances of those about him. It is Jennings's uncomfortably visible juxtaposition of East and West, elements that otherwise seem (or are hoped to be) incompatible with one another, that makes him so disconcerting to the English community around Frizinghall, which wears the face of the internally consistent, pure English character. As Jennings examines the English countenance from the perspective of an other, he finds "a wonderful sameness in the solid expression of the English face" just as "there is a wonderful sameness in the solid side of the English character" (469), and it is this internal uniformity, this "sameness" that he himself so detrimentally lacks. But this coherence turns out to be absent even where Jennings thinks he finds it, in the English face and character, as the motley national character of Franklin Blake illustrates. And Blake's nationally mixed personality is itself only a particularly blatant symptom of a more subtle lack of continuity in the surrounding English culture that is frequently associated in the novel with Indian admixtures, as is evident both in the Indian cultural traces that can be seen in the English domestic scene of the novel and in the ease with which Indian people and objects circulate within English culture and society.

"Your Indian Cabinet Has No Lock to It"

The most overtly foregrounded of these Indian admixtures to show itself in the English domestic environment is of course the Moonstone itself, but even it is effortlessly assimilated, for while its presence is viewed implicitly as an exception, it is an exception that is fully embraced rather than rejected: Rachel Verinder literally takes the diamond to her breast, wearing it "as a brooch in the bosom of her white dress" (100). But embraced or not, Rachel's Indian diamond is not even as much of an exception as it may at first appear, for it soon finds a home inside yet another Indian object that has assumed an unexceptionable position in her English home, "an Indian cabinet which stood in her sitting-room" (112). The exotic gem thus takes its rather mundane place amongst the Indian cabinets, shawls, and other Indian accessories that typically adorn the fashionable woman's home and body. The Indian cabinet also serves importantly as a point of reference for the respective roles of putatively English elements and Indian admixtures in English culture. When Lady Verinder objects of her daughter's storage place for the gem that "your Indian cabinet has no lock to it" (112), her reservation is ironically readable in at least two ways: either she fears that the absence of a lock means that the Moonstone might more easily be stolen (the more obvious reading), or she is afraid that the Indian diamond's mysterious influence will not be sufficiently contained by an unlocked cabinet. Either way, her fears prove justified, for the diamond indeed turns up missing soon after being placed in the cabinet, and its freedom from containment wreaks havoc in the lives of all it has touched. The leaky Indian cabinet is thus implicitly contrasted against the previous two staunch repositories of the gem, "the safe keeping of a bank in London" and "the safe keeping of the bank at Frizinghall" (77). The English bank functions as the paradigm of security, for even the relentless Brahmins themselves are daunted enough by it to make no attempt on the diamond as long as it resides there. The contrast between English bank and Indian cabinet thus paints English institutions as more stable and reliable than their Indian equivalents—if the Indian counterparts can indeed be called equivalents, for the difference in scale between the Indian cabinet and the English bank in fact underscores that there is at the time no comparable Indian institution, no "Bank of India" to complete the implicit analogy.

If the English bank is the gold standard of security, though, it is security only of a specific kind: that which answers to the first interpretation of Lady Verinder's reluctance to allow the diamond to be stored in the Indian cabinet (that is, for fear it will be stolen). With respect to the second construction one might place on her apprehensiveness (that is, a fear that the Indian diamond's influence might seep its way out of its supposed containment), the Moonstone's residence in the English bank arguably represents the worst case scenario, for if Rachel Verinder's wearing of the diamond as a brooch in the bosom of her white dress is representative at a domestic level of a putatively pure English culture literally taking a dangerous Indian influence to its breast, then the English bank's hermetic enclosure of the diamond represents the same process at a collective institutional level. Even the idea of safety from theft is problematic, however, for there is a clash between the particularity of individual requirements for security on one hand and the monumental impersonality of the bank as an institution on the other. Although "the safe keeping of a bank in London" is the ne plus ultra of security against the Verinders' losing possession of the diamond, it is ironically in a London bank that the Moonstone in fact resides for most of the time that the Verinders regard it as missing, having been deposited there by a pawnbroker who took it in pledge from the thief. The bank thus provides security only at a blind and impersonal level, for it has no detailed concern for, nor even awareness of, competing individual claims of ownership, which are after all at the very heart of the notion of security for the individuals in question.

This apparent indifference verges over into competing claims of ownership, however, when the actions of the thief himself suggest that the delusively comforting bank is perhaps even dangerously *self*-interested. It comes to light when the mystery is finally solved that it was Godfrey Ablewhite, son and implicit representative of a prominent London banker, who pawned the gem after the opium-besotted Franklin Blake handed him the diamond saying "take it back, Godfrey, to your father's bank. It's safe there—it's not safe here" (510). Young Godfrey's unreliability takes on suggestive racial-national overtones as well, for although the name of Ablewhite sets him up as the supposedly adept Westerner—the "able white" as opposed perhaps to the ostensibly incompetent dark races of the British colonies—this able white is in fact a sham, presenting every outward indication of trustworthiness and competence but underhandedly betraying his compatriots' faith. Squandering various trusts placed in him as the supposedly responsible heir to a respected London banking interest (he also embezzles £20,000 from a young man for whom he has been appointed trustee), Ablewhite suggests a fundamental unreliability at the heart of the English bank.

It is the nonwhites who instead turn out to be the able ones, for just as the English bank was contrasted against the Indian cabinet, so is the ineffectiveness of the English who wish to maintain possession of the Moonstone juxtaposed against the finely honed competence of the Indian Brahmins, whose proficiency becomes evident in all of their barely visible attempts to retrieve the Moonstone. For instance, the pawnbroker to whom Ablewhite pledges the diamond in London finds that an immigrant Hindu in his employ has nearly succeeded in stealing the gem in secret cooperation with the three Brahmins. In fact, in addition to their facility at negotiating business and social situations such as the chief's meeting with the lawyer Bruff, the Brahmins even have an "organization" in London consisting of "the command of money; the services, when needed, of that shady sort of Englishman, who lives in the byeways of foreign life in London; and lastly, the secret sympathy of such few men of their country, and (formerly, at least) of their own religion, as happen to be employed in ministering to some of the multitudinous wants of this great city" (330–31). The specific character of the organization makes it evident that the Indians' effectiveness is due not only to their unexpected adeptness with British culture but also to the degree to which the Brahmins and their compatriots are integral elements of that culture. Their success is also due to their awareness of, and ability to exploit, the discontinuities in the British character, such as the at best qualified Englishness of "that shady sort of Englishman, who lives in the byeways of foreign life in London."

By the close of *The Moonstone,* all of the most obvious manifestations of this interwoven Indian culture have been tidily swept off the scene one way or another: the Brahmins have gone back to their homeland, taking the Moonstone with them, Ezra Jennings has succumbed to his terminal illness, and even Mr. Murthwaite has departed for another expedition to India. It seems almost as if Collins means to reassure his readers that these hybrid Anglo-Indian bogeymen were wheeled onto the stage only for this performance and are now, in Thackeray style, safely shut away again. But what of the pervasive English susceptibility to the hypnotic influence of Indian cultural traces? Is it realistic to presume that the fascinations have disappeared along with their objects? (For that matter, the Indian cabinet, the Indian employees of pawnbrokers, and other such exotic traces have presumably not disappeared.) And what of the fact that even the English characters who remain in England all seem to fit Detective Sergeant Cuff's description of Godfrey Ablewhite, whose "life had two sides to it" (506), especially when the second sides of those lives are all tied in one way or another to India? Ablewhite's second side, for instance, shows itself only under the disguise of "a noticeably dark complexion" that causes his pursuers at first to mistake him for one of the Brahmins (487, 500). Franklin Blake's various faces include, as we have seen, occasional reversions to the character of a wanderer in the East, and he has a buried separate consciousness that emerges only under the influence of opium, a commodity rife with Indian connotations. Indeed the very paradigm of purity in the novel, Rachel Verinder herself, leads something of a double life that makes her complicit in Franklin Blake's opium-induced alien consciousness for the majority of the novel, as she persistently refuses to divulge her knowledge of his actions on the evening that he took the Moonstone from her room. The union between the two that gives the novel its comedic resolution in fact only insures that this mixed identity will characterize yet another generation.[14]

All this is as much as to say that *The Moonstone* raises far more specters of a hybrid Anglo-Indian culture than it finally lays to rest. In this respect it aptly represents late-century English culture, for such fears came to be an integral and overt part of a British imperial consciousness by the century's last decades, as is evident in perhaps the most noted expression of a British ideology of imperialism, Sir John Seeley's 1883 series of lectures published as *The Expansion of England*. "Do we suppose," Seeley ominously asked, ". . . that in the next century, if the colonial . . . connection has been maintained and has become closer, England itself will not be very much modified and transformed?" *The Moonstone* anticipates such trepidation by fifteen years, but with the additional insight that the modification Seeley *foresees* has, in the culture Collins's novel portrays, *long been underway,* even though Britons have been blind—perhaps willfully blind—to the process. Just as Franklin Blake arrogantly and mistakenly searches *around* himself for the thief of the Moonstone only to find the culprit *inside* himself in the end, so do Britons deludedly locate India in the East only to find that it is after all an inextricable part of their culture at home. Although Collins does not necessarily raise an alarm, he does evince a certain uneasiness in his representations of English people reduced to willess, hypnotized children before the seductive allure of various Indian cultural traces. And it is opium that both symbolizes and manifests this hypnotic effect on a putatively physiological level that parallels the cultural one, and that once again, as in the case of De Quincey, brings to the surface the hidden Oriental character buried within supposedly English culture.

V

"The Plague Spreading and
Attacking Our Vitals"

*The Victorian Opium Den
and Oriental Contagion*

IN 1883, the Reverend George Piercy, a former missionary to Canton, added
his voice to an increasingly vocal movement to end the Indo-Chinese opium
trade with a warning about what he viewed as the inevitable consequences of
the rising incidence of opium smoking in England:[1]

> *With great pain of mind, I now must say evidence clearly and strongly shows
> that we really have a new habit, prolific of evil, springing up amongst us. . . .
> It is coming close to us with a rapidity and spring almost undreamt of even by
> those who have dreaded its stealthy and unseen step. . . . There have been
> warning voices in the air, but they have been little heeded. Those who have
> been claiming justice for China relative to the opium traffic at the hands of our
> government have not been silent on this point—the reflex action and retributive
> consequence of our own doings. . . . What could all this grow to but to the
> plague spreading and attacking our vitals? If I speak again of what has been seen
> of the Chinese who smoke opium in London it must be understood that it is
> to raise a warning voice against the evil they have brought. It begins with the
> Chinese, but does not end with them![2]*

Piercy says outright at the end of the century what Coleridge implied at its
beginning: as retribution for England's dishonorable imperial policies ("the re-
flex action and retributive consequence of our own doings"), the Orient (especially China) will enter, colonize, and conquer the English body in the form of
a contaminating contagion enabled by opium.

Piercy's greater explicitness is a function of several factors related to his
professional and historical situations. As a member of the increasingly defined
and strongly evangelical anti-opium movement, for instance, he predictably resorts to a familiar rhetoric characterizing opium as the agent of rampant sin and
an overall slide into perdition.[3] And, like many other missionaries to China, he
would undoubtedly have been stung by the criticism the Chinese commonly

leveled against missionaries there—that the opium trade was inconsistent with Christianity—and his warning perhaps evinces an eagerness to vindicate his own integrity by heralding his opposition to such un-Christian practices. He probably also shared a resentment born of an impression common among missionaries that the opium trade, over and above its ideological inconsistencies, was a hindrance to the missionary's daily work, that the slow pace of Christianizing the Chinese was due to the prevalence among them of addiction to opium smoking, by far the preferred means of using the drug in China then.[4] In addition to personal and professional factors, there had been significant historical changes with respect to the putative separation between England and its Oriental colonies since the time of "Kubla Khan" and the *Confessions of an English Opium-Eater,* changes that would have fueled the sense of urgency behind Piercy's warning. Most notably, the Chinese population in England had been growing rapidly over the previous three decades—from a meager 78 in England and Wales in 1851 to 665 by 1881, with a sudden dramatic increase in the mid-1860s according to contemporary census reports.[5] Despite the Chinese community's small share of the total population, it caused widespread anxieties in England paralleling concurrent hysteria about the "yellow peril" in the United States, Australia, and New Zealand, to which Chinese workers were emigrating by the thousands.[6] In addition to a predictable suspicion of immigrants—the familiar dynamic in which natives become hostile to perceived interlopers with whom they must compete for jobs and resources[7]—English fears were exacerbated by a vague anticipation of retribution for the "doings" to which Piercy alludes: the Empire's controversial opium-trading practices with China.

Even apart from its imaginable vendetta, however, China was potentially threatening for other reasons. Characterizing itself as a superior nation above the "barbarian" ones of the West, the Celestial Empire was easy to see as a rival to the growing British Empire. Even though it was behindhand in military technology, China boasted (as De Quincey had nervously noted earlier) a huge population and a culture that seemed to have persisted largely unchanged for thousands of years. The mere existence of such a rival empire predictably incited fears of at best competition for territories, at worst a reversal of British colonization of the Orient. Fears of such a reversal were reinforced by the steamship, which had been a decisive factor in British imperial expansion in the East during the era of "gunboat imperialism" in India and China,[8] for by the 1860s the steamship was also the chief means of introducing Orientals to England as the Blue Funnel Line and other newly established merchant steamer operations between England and the East employed Oriental seamen by the hundreds. In fact the majority of Orientals in England were seamen living in the dock districts of London and Liverpool.[9] Thus the same advance in technology that had brought the English to the Orient was now bringing Orientals en masse to England. Even barring fears of full-fledged reverse colonization, this influx of peoples from the colonies would have been jarring for its disruption of the widely accepted model of a well-demarcated British Empire with its center in London and its periphery in (among other places) the Orient.

I begin with Piercy because his fears that England will be infected through opium smoking are representative of a broad-based trend in the last third of the nineteenth century: when the supposedly vindictive Chinese and other Orientals immigrating to England were fitted in the popular consciousness with what Edward Said calls "the nineteenth-century academic and imaginative demonology of 'the mysterious Orient,'"[10] the result was an enemy who could be expected to use subtle and evil means to gain the field and to bide his time and endure privations in doing so. Such perceptions are reflected not only in the explicitly anti-opium press in which Piercy's warning appears but also in a new literary genre that evolved through the last three and a half decades of the century and consisted of narratives about mysterious and evil opium dens in the East End of London, a region itself repeatedly figured as a miniature Orient within the heart of the empire.[11] Modern audiences are still acquainted with the genre mainly through the fiction of Dickens, Wilde, Conan Doyle, and early twentieth-century British popular fiction.[12] But even before nineteenth-century readers entered these authors' fictional dens, they were veterans of the East End and its opium establishments, having vicariously traversed the narrow alleyways of Bluegate Fields in countless magazines, newspapers, and books presenting reports from "roving correspondents" who had taken the then fashionable police-guided tour of the East End and its dens—a common practice known familiarly at the time as "doing the slums."[13] From its inception, the genre was intensely formulaic, and the formulae all point to anxieties about an Oriental infection as insidious invasion, a fear of which Piercy's warning is an especially obvious index. It is not surprising that the fear is most closely associated with the Chinese, who had especially charged historical ties to both England and opium. Indeed opium smoking was assumed to be so essentially Chinese that the practice is portrayed in the narratives as having the capacity gradually to render Britons more Chinese in their customs, attitudes, and physical appearance.[14]

The specific means by which opium supposedly transmits this infection are varied. Sometimes the seductiveness and will-usurping quality of the drug are implicitly portrayed as enabling Oriental men to gain sexual power over Englishwomen, thus setting the stage for anxieties about racial purity, fears that were exacerbated by growing apprehensions that the increased mixing of cultures and races in the British Empire would dissipate British identity and undermine England's control of the empire. But the contagion is more often portrayed as being communicated by inhalation of the opium smoke itself, without

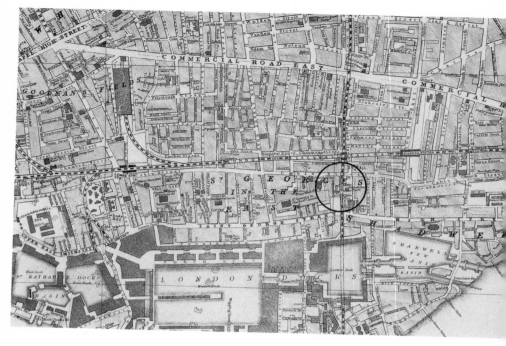

Figure 1. London's Dock District in the late nineteenth century, western portion. Just east of the Tower of London, this area was the home of Oriental sailors who came and went via the nearby docks. Bluegate Fields, the most commonly invoked site of opium dens, appears here under its newer name, Victoria Street, juxtaposed with the railroad tracks in the circled area. (*New Large-Scale Ordnance Atlas of London and Suburbs.* London: George W. Bacon, 1888. Courtesy of the Lilly Library, Indiana University, Bloomington.)

any other physical contact between English and Oriental. Orientalness is thus portrayed as a transmittable disease, and opium smoke as the means of transmission. So when Piercy speaks of "the plague spreading and attacking our vitals," he does not necessarily refer only or even primarily to an increased incidence of addiction to opium smoking; he instead anticipates a more comprehensive infectious Chineseness eating away at the very identity of England and its people.

"The Woman Has Opium-Smoked Herself into a Strange Likeness of the Chinaman"

Although the opium den narrative arguably came into its own with Dickens's *The Mystery of Edwin Drood* (1870), the genre had been gestating for years in

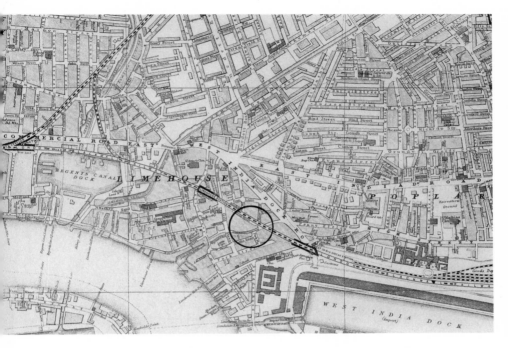

Figure 2. London's Dock District in the late nineteenth century, eastern portion. Abutting the eastern edge of figure 1, this region includes Limehouse, a predominantly Chinese ghetto into the twentieth century. Limehouse Causeway (crossing the railroad tracks in the circled area) was another frequently cited locale of opium dens in late-century accounts.(*New Large-Scale Ordnance Atlas of London and Suburbs*. London: George W. Bacon, 1888. Courtesy of the Lilly Library, Indiana University, Bloomington.)

a handful of popular magazines before Dickens tried his hand at it. In fact Dickens's interest in the topic was probably sparked by an article he published in his own journal *All the Year Round* in 1866. The article, "Lazarus, Lotus-Eating," is a present-tense, first-person-plural narrative of a slumming expedition to an East End "opium divan" and is one of the first published portrayals of an opium den. It already exhibits at least two characteristics that were to become standard features of the genre: (1) an almost superstitious dread of Orientals and a tendency to portray them as animals and/or vampirelike living dead parasites and (2) a preoccupation with the role of Englishwomen in the opium den accompanied by the suggestion that they are being Orientalized and assimilated.

The narrator describes Lazarus (his nickname for a Chinese beggar "we" follow to an opium den) as "one of the poor wretched Chinamen who shiver and cower and whine at our street-corners, and are mean and dirty, squalid and contemptible, even beyond beggars generally."[15] This distaste is equivocally shared by "Mr. Policeman," who scoffs at "them Chinamen," who "beg, and duff, and dodge about the West End—we won't have 'em here—and never spend nothin' of what they makes, till night." On one hand, the officer seems to suspect that these foreigners do not really need the money they beg. But, on the other hand, he grudgingly admires their restraint in spending their money, a symptom of an almost superhuman ability to endure privation and defer gratification. "They don't care for no drink and seem to live without eating, so far as I know," he says. The gratification they enjoy at last, however, provides a foothold for defensive contempt, and he patronizingly paints the Oriental beggars as fuzzy little animals piled atop one another in their den: "It's their opium at night they likes, and you'll find half a dozen on 'em in one bed at Yahee's a-smoking and sleeping away, like so many dormice!"[16]

The narrator is similarly conflicted, for he seems irresistibly drawn even as he is repulsed, going to considerable trouble to track Lazarus back to his den, where he then keenly scrutinizes him and other members of his Oriental community. Even though he assures us beforehand that "there is no limit to the variety of nationalities patronizing the wretched hovel we are about to visit," one would not know it from his description once we get there, for he focuses exclusively on Orientals, all of them vampirelike or animalistic. The scene consists of

> the livid, cadaverous, corpse-like visage of Yahee, the wild excited glare of the young Lascar who opens the door, the stolid sheep-like ruminations of Lazarus and the other Chinamen coiled together on the floor, the incoherent anecdotes of the old Bengalee squatted on the bed, the fiery gesticulations of the mulatto and the Manilla-man who are in conversation by the fire, the semi-idiotic jabber of the negroes huddled up behind Yahee, [and] the bearded Oriental, who makes faces and passes jibes at, and for, the company.[17]

These Orientals seem about to burst into violence with their wild excited glares and fiery gesticulations, but their smoldering aggression is ultimately channeled instead through the tools and products of opium smoking—a sublimation especially evident in the case of one Oriental smoker who "looks a little dangerous as he brandishes his opium pipe." Even the very air in the den is threatening as the opium fumes exercise an insidious power over the English reporter: "The cramped little chamber is one large opium-pipe, and inhaling its atmosphere partly brings you under the pipe's influence."[18] An earlier account of what seems to be the same den more vividly describes the smoke's peculiarly Oriental and oppressive quality, leaving the impression that it imprisons the breather in what otherwise might have been a luxurious Oriental pleasure binge: "the fumes gather in intensity, and though we sit near the opened door, it is not without an oppressed feeling about the head—as if the crowning towel of a Turkish bath had petrified, after being more than ever tightly bound over the temples."[19]

The smoke's insinuating influence seems already to have gained a grip on Yahee's next-door neighbors, three Englishwomen. The presence of women in the dens at all disrupts an implicit convention, for as the narrator of "Lazarus" has said, "from every quarter of the globe, and more immediately from every district in London, *men* come to old Yahee" (my emphasis),[20] and the narrator of the earlier account, who finds an English woman merely "lean[ing] against the doorpost" of this same den insists that "the woman has no business there."[21] But these women not only enter the den, they have in fact been so drawn into its Oriental culture that they are now known only by the half-Oriental nicknames of "Mother Abdallah," "Cheeny (China) Emma," and "Lascar Sal." "I've lived here these dozen year, and naturally have got into many of their ways," says Mother Abdallah of her Oriental neighbors, implying that it is inevitable and not necessarily regrettable that Oriental attributes should rub off on Westerners if only they are exposed to them for long enough.[22]

The earlier account of the same den discusses this inevitable Orientalization in greater detail, linking it more explicitly to the influence of opium and taking a more negative view of it. The earlier reporter tells of Mother Abdallah's cohort, "'Cheeney Emma,' who lives next door but one, and who, from long consorting with Chinamen, has acquired their habits and 'cries fit to kill herself' when deprived of her daily pabulum of opium."[23] An explorer of another den even seems to detect traces of a programmatic conspiracy mounted by pusher-like Orientals to hook Englishwomen: "When asked how she came to take to opium-smoking, [Eliza, the wife of "a black-moustached, swarthy Lascar"] says that she can speak Hindi and Hindustani, and used to be with those that spoke them, and one would say to her, 'Have a whiff,' and another would say to her, 'Have a whiff,' and she knew no better, and so she got into the habit, and now she cannot leave it off."[24]

These scenes of assimilation are particularly charged, for not only are English subjects Orientalized but, specifically, Englishwomen are subsumed by Oriental men. Yet another reporter is similarly fascinated by this phenomenon, focusing on a Chinese opium master's English wife, who "looks as though she is being gradually smoke-dried, and by and by will present the appearance of an Egyptian mummy."[25] To be hooked into opium smoking is thus not only to be made more Chinese but to be exiled to a sort of life-in-death. The Englishwoman here is drained of both English identity and vitality as she is

Figure 3. "In the Den." A graphic representation of the stereotyped Chinese opium smokers who become the touchstone for the Orientalization of English smokers. ("A Night in an Opium Den," *Strand Magazine* 1 [1891]. Photograph by Donna Hall)

"smoke-dried" and made to appear like the Oriental archetype of life-in-death, the indefinitely preserved corpse of the Egyptian mummy. In this too she is made more like the opium master, for the narrator of "Lazarus" similarly says of Yahee that "his sunken eyes, fallen cheeks, cadaverous parchment-like skin, and deathly whiteness, make him resemble a hideous and long-forgotten mummy."[26]

Yet another observer finds a different opium master's English wife so extensively transformed that

> it was only by her speech that her nationality could be so readily decided. A small lean woman, with such a marvellous grafting of Chinese about her, that her cotton gown of English cut seemed to hang awkwardly on her sharp shoulders. Her skin was dusky yellow, and tightly drawn at the nostrils and the cheekbones; and evidently she had, since her marriage, taken such an Oriental

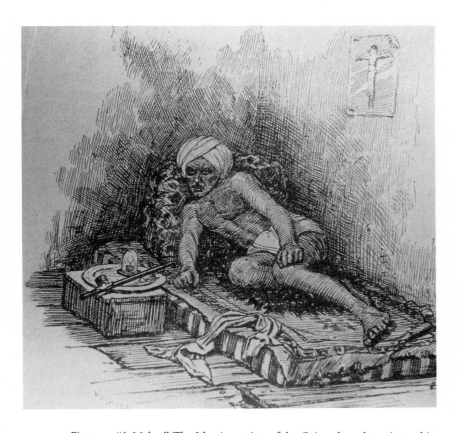

Figure 4. "A Malay." The Islamic version of the Oriental smoker, pictured in an ambiguous reclining position (in repose or in a catlike crouch?), has threateningly clenched fists and furrowed brow. Lying nearly naked in the foreground, he bears a jarring resemblance to the image of the crucifixion hanging above him in the background, a point of Western reference that fails to provide the perhaps usually expected contrast here ("A Night in an Opium Den," *Strand Magazine* 1 [1891]. Photograph by Donna Hall)

view of life, that her organs of vision were fast losing their European shape, and assuming that which coincided with her adopted nature. She was very ill, poor woman. It was killing her, she said, this constant breathing of the fumes of the subtle drug her husband dealt in.[27]

Again the opium-smoked Englishwoman is Orientalized and suspended between life and death. These narrators all share a morbid sense of awe at the vampirelike power the Chinese opium master wields through his opium, the smoke of which apparently enables him not only to attract Englishwomen but to assimilate them, to convert them into something living-dead and Oriental like himself.

Such notions of Oriental men absconding with Englishwomen were ubiquitous during the last quarter of the century. A series of popular ballads published during and immediately after the shah of Persia's visit to Victoria, for instance, consistently jokes that the shah is sexually insatiable and means to steal a crowd of Englishwomen for his harem. "When the shah returns, take home he will, / Seven hundred wives from saffron hill," says one,[28] while another warns that

> He wants 500 English girls,
> To please him night and day,
> So married men look after your wives,
> Or he'll take them all away.[29]

The shah falls prey here to the stereotype of Oriental men as insatiable sexual athletes,[30] and like the Chinese opium master, he has tastes that run to the necrophilic, showing a preference for mummylike Western women:

> To Madame Tussaud's the shah he went, at the mummies he did stare,
> He felt them all, though not alive, the wax work girls so fair.[31]

This concern that foreign men will assimilate Englishwomen, though it is in the form of a joke in these ballads, recurs with greater seriousness in the literature of late century, such as Bram Stoker's *Dracula,* which elaborates the anxiety specifically in the form of the fear that living-dead foreigners will colonize England by subsuming all of its women and making them invincible living-dead monsters like themselves.[32] The recurrent pattern evokes age-old anxieties related to exogamy, the practice in which women of one cultural or social group marry men of another. As Robin Fox says, "groups speaking the same language and being alike in other ways might well exchange wives among themselves—but the connubium stopped at the boundaries of language, territory, or colour, or whatever marked 'us' off from 'them.'"[33] Such anxieties are closely linked to the fear of racial dilution, for if members of markedly different social groups are allowed to crossbreed, then the differences that supposedly demarcate group identity will begin to dissolve. The connubial boundary is particularly charged when the groups in question are overtly at odds, for its breach would then make it impossible to sort family members from enemies. Anxieties about exogamy have been a recurrent feature of patriarchal societies at least since the days of the Hebrew Bible, but they were exacerbated in late-nineteenth-century England by the heightened stakes of separating "us" from "them" entailed in the imperial project then approaching its zenith. Britons in mid- to late century might have looked down on an Englishwoman who married an American man, for instance, but in the wake of the opium wars they would have been likely to view a liaison between an Englishwoman and a Chinese man with outright fear.

It is not only fear of genetic contamination that drives the imperial anxieties around exogamy, however, for they are also fueled by Victorian English attitudes that at once devalue and enthrone the feminine. As has often been noted, a hegemonic Victorian middle-class sensibility conceived of woman as the "angel in the house," the rearer of children, the executor of the household—in short, the center of domestic existence. Thus women were effectively marginalized and centralized at once, for domestic pursuits were typically trivialized in comparison to the supposedly more substantial and consequential masculine ones such as government, commerce, military campaigns, and so on. But insofar as this same sensibility emphasized the household and the family as the backbone of English character, women were empowered—or at least femininity was reified as an important national resource over which women exerted primary, local control, even if they did not dictate the terms by which that resource was incorporated into a larger social picture. "As guardian of the private sphere," says Lynda Nead, "woman was believed to play an essential part in the construction and perpetuation of domestic social order," and "the establishment and maintenance of the domestic unit was the basis for social stability and order."[34] Mary Poovey similarly notes that the nineteenth-century middle-class ideal Englishwoman "taught her children a morality centered on discipline and self-control; in doing so she helped promote the values necessary to another generation of successful competitors."[35] The sentiment is summed up by Samuel Smiles: "The Home is the crystal of society—the very nucleus of national character; and from that source, be it pure or tainted, issue the habits, principles and maxims, which govern public as well as private life. The Nation comes from the nursery; public opinion itself is for the most part the outgrowth of the home."[36]

It follows from this line of reasoning that it would be all-important for Englishwomen to be paired with the right men—and, of course, *English*men—in order for the English character to maintain its strength, its integrity, its very definition. Otherwise children would presumably be reared in "tainted" homes and would manifest a corrupt "national character." This apprehensiveness about domestic purity joins with anxieties about genetic contamination to undergird the fears around the miscegenative dynamics of the opium den, for to control

Englishwomen is indirectly to control the domestic environment, and to control the domestic environment is to control "the habits, principles and maxims, which govern public as well as private life"—that is, the society at large.

"Some Contagion in Them Seizes upon Him"

Any argument about the role of women in these narratives necessarily proceeds at a serious disadvantage, however, for none of the accounts published before *The Mystery of Edwin Drood* (1870) present English*men* in similar circumstances as points of comparison. It is true that the narrators and their companions are implicitly male, but they merely enter the scene temporarily as ostensibly detached observers, and if they do smoke opium, they are not shown doing it. Although the narrators of several accounts written in 1870 and after describe their experiences of smoking opium, none of the accounts published before *Edwin Drood* feature opium-smoking men, narrators or otherwise. One might view the exclusively female English characters as synecdoches for a feminized England in general—as another implicit expression of the belief that the defining attributes of the nation are those associated with femininity and domestic values. In this light, the women might even be seen as a propagandistic whitewash of the British colonial superpower. After all, much of what is typically regarded as negative about the stance of British imperial government toward its subjects—strict discipline, domineering control, and so forth—is stereotypically masculine and paternal and is perhaps rendered more positive and seemingly benevolent by identification instead with clichéd maternal values, especially when the English maternal values are contrasted against those of the coarse, violent, and possibly evil Oriental men of the opium den.[37]

What we see in these opium dens, however, is not a strong feminine Britain asserting its virtuous, nurturing values against a negative, implicitly masculine Oriental influence. Instead we see weak women whose identities are subsumed by Oriental men. Perhaps these authors were anticipating Rev. Piercy with veiled expressions of fears that the colonial process was collapsing, even turning itself inside out as strong Orientals came to prey upon a dissipated England. One social critic indicts England's moral degradation not only as the chink in the armor that allows Orientals to gain entry to England but as one of the chief attractions that makes them want to come in the first place:

> *Our streets . . . are so infected with vice . . . that we are, and have been, the astonishment of our Oriental visitors, and the remark of all Foreigners, many of whom, and we feel indignant at merely writing it, openly announce, "that while they love not our climate, customs, or manners, adore our women, and cannot away from them!" . . . We fear they have, from such sights, during their*

visits to England, come to very unfavorable conclusions regarding our Christian *Women here . . . and pronounce them not only "fair," but so adapted to their vile purposes that they come far and wide to revel in them, and to sink them into the lowest depths of death.*[38]

It is significantly not just moral degradation in the abstract that lures these foreigners, but rather the particular sexuality that is supposedly peculiar to Englishwomen. The idea begins to take shape here that Englishwomen are not just an asset to be protected against foreign infection; they seem also—or perhaps even instead—to be a liability that attracts and enables that infection in the first place, not only of their own individual bodies but also of the collective British body.

During this same period, women were similarly scapegoated as the source of another dangerous contagion in the discourse that surrounded one of the most controversial pieces of legislation of the 1860s. Intended to control the skyrocketing incidence of venereal disease among English military personnel, the Contagious Diseases Act of 1864 instituted regulation of prostitutes near several military bases in England by providing that "any Superintendent or Inspector of Police or Constabulary authorized to act in that Place, having good Cause to believe that [a] common Prostitute has a Contagious Disease, may . . . take her into Custody" and forcibly confine her in a hospital until she is "cured."[39] Opponents of the bill objected chiefly to its flagrant abridgement of Englishwomen's personal freedoms. But, surprisingly enough, no one seemed to take issue with the fundamental reasoning behind that abridgement. Even critics of the bill appeared to agree that women were responsible for the spreading infection insofar as they were supposed to be uniquely able to halt its progress. A sermon by the Reverend Fulwar William Fowle, for instance, preaches against the denial of "the innate privileges, and the rightful protection of a free-born daughter of Britain." But his defence does not take the tack of indignation at the unjust scapegoating of the Englishwoman; instead he opts for Christian advocacy of her as a sinner deserving mercy: "Our sister has fallen. But she is our sister still; a baptized child of God, with the sign of the cross upon her forehead, which guilt has not erased." He slaps Parliament's wrist for punishing "our sister" but not for finding her guilty. And his alternative solution to the legislation further buys into its reasoning as he exhorts Englishwomen to behave themselves on their own. "Foremost among the weak things which God makes powerful is *Female Influence,*" he says; "Then, what a responsibility does it involve! . . . women of England, you may take your stand and stay the plague."[40]

The trouble presumably starts—or at least continues—when women do not "take their stand," when they stray from their proper role as angels in the house. Of course tradition has it that the widest divergence from the angel role is that of the whore, and supporters and opponents of the Contagious Diseases Act alike agree that it is prostitutes who are most threatening. But their menace is by no means limited to their function as more or less passive carriers of infection. This is especially true of "man-trappers" in the East End of London, who are consistently characterized in the slumming accounts as dangerously active beasts of prey. One East End explorer describes the area of the dock district most noted for, besides its opium dens, a particularly dangerous species of "she creature":

> Only such of the public as are accustomed to read the daily papers can form any idea as to the kind of place Bluegate Fields is. Commonly it is known as "Tiger Bay," on account of the number of ferocious she creatures in petticoats that lurk and lair there. . . . The inhabitants of Bluegate Fields are the worst in England, consisting of man-trappers for the shipping lying in the river just below, and the tigresses before mentioned, who inveigle tipsy sailors from the many surrounding abominable dens "licensed for dancing and music," and drug them and strip and rob and ill use them.[41]

These "tigresses," as it turns out, are a threat not just to tipsy sailors but to men of any class and occupation. The self-consciously well-dressed middle-class narrator of an anonymous *Strand* article recounts being ogled by one of them: "Beginning at my boots, and travelling up by way of trousers and waistcoat, up to my collar and face, she examined me so critically and searchingly from head to foot that I fancied once or twice I could see the row of figures she was inwardly casting up." He awakens from an opium debauch sans boots, hat, and umbrella.[42] Another slumming correspondent paints a less cartoonish scene of greater danger with his recollection that "the stranger who ventured alone after ten or eleven o'clock through any of the streets between the [Ratcliff] 'Highway' and Cable Street was almost certain to be hustled and robbed [by "the gorgeous array of the insatiable she-creatures who turned out at nightfall to seek their prey in the streets and public-houses"], nor could the police, who patrolled their beats in twos and sometimes threes, ensure any man's safety."[43]

These stereotypes of dangerous East End women merge with familiar miscegenation anxieties in Dickens's *The Mystery of Edwin Drood* (1870). Following in the footsteps of the magazine correspondents, Dickens's narrator views the Oriental opium smokers in the den of the novel's opening scene as animalistic, violent, and vaguely evil: "[The] Chinaman convulsively wrestles with one of his many Gods, or devils, perhaps, and snarls horribly," while "the Lascar laughs and dribbles at the mouth" (38).[44] And once again an Englishwoman's opium smoking in proximity to these Oriental beast-men is associated with a contagious Oriental identity: "The woman has opium-smoked herself into a strange likeness of the Chinaman. His form of cheek, eye, and temple, and his color are repeated in her" (38). But Dickens also throws a new curve: having caught the Oriental bug, this woman in turn threatens to infect an English*man*, John Jasper, who also smokes in the den: "As he watches the spasmodic shoots and darts that break out of her face and limbs, like fitful lightning out of a dark sky, some contagion in them seizes upon him: insomuch that he has to withdraw himself to a lean armchair by the hearth—placed there, perhaps, for such emergencies—and to sit in it, holding tight, until he has got the better of this unclean spirit of imitation" (39). By making an Englishwoman the immediate source of this "unclean spirit," Dickens goes a step further with the uneasiness about contact between Englishwomen and Oriental men. What is at stake here is no longer only the insidiously Orientalizing influence of the opium den over Englishwomen; instead, like supporters of the Contagious Diseases Act, Dickens's narrator is perhaps even more concerned about the consequences with respect to Englishmen of the contagion of which these women seem to have become carriers.[45]

Maternity in the Marketplace

It is against the backdrop of calculatingly rapacious East End prostitutes that Dickens's Princess Puffer comes into relief. The dockside prostitutes are fearsome in part for the dangerous contagions they carry, and Princess Puffer is much like them in this respect. But the man-trapping tigress is frightening also because she has a profit motive where her maternal heart should be. Worse yet, her profit is always a man's loss, and she is ruthlessly efficient in the pursuit of her goal. Whereas the ideal angel in the house is a selfless mother figure driven to sacrifice herself for her charges and moves only in the domestic realm whose purity she guards, the prostitute is the inversion of that fantasy, operating exclusively in the tainted world of commerce and driven to sacrifice her charges to self-interest. Princess Puffer is like her neighbors in this respect as well, for she competes successfully in the opium-smoking marketplace traditionally dominated by Oriental men, operating an opium den patronized by several Oriental customers as well as the Englishman John Jasper. And her success seems due largely to a savvy manipulation of the middle-class ideals of femininity that paradoxically both empower and disenfranchise women. She exploits expectations around the angel in the house role to commercial advantage, claiming to take a maternal interest in her customers that her nearest competitor cannot share. "Well," she says, "there's land customers, and there's water customers. I'm a mother to both. Different to Jack Chinaman t'other side the court. He ain't a father to neither. It ain't in him" (266).

Never mind that as a man "Jack Chinaman" cannot possibly be a mother; Princess Puffer insists that he cannot be a father either, for "it ain't in him." He lacks any nurturing capacity and so loses the game without even having known its rules. The question is now not one of traditionally masculine knowledge, technological superiority, and so on, but instead one of conventionally feminine abilities such as nurturance. According to Nead, "maternal love was constructed [by the middle classes] as the apex of feminine purity, and as an unattainable model for all other human relationships."[46] Princess Puffer's edge is to have attained at least the illusion of this ideal model in another human relationship, and a commercial one at that. She manages to exploit the centrality of traditionally feminine attributes in one realm (maternal nurturance in the household) in order to wield power in another context in which those attributes are usually seen as alien and inferior (the marketplace). She thus breaks down the cultural division between "the respective domains of domestic woman and economic man" that was initially constructed by eighteenth-century conduct manuals and persisted well into the nineteenth century.[47] And by importing this apex of feminine purity to her opium den, she glosses over the contagion and moral degradation typically associated with that scene—and perhaps especially the women in it—thus sliding across the supposed boundary between purity and contamination as well.

But, unsurprisingly, Dickens does not present this mercantile empowerment of a woman as positive. Rather, Princess Puffer's manipulation of archetypal images and values associated with femininity is at best disingenuous, at worst sinister. She herself certainly does not conform to the image she manipulates, for she is far from the ideal middle-class mother as domestic angel, being more akin to the stock Dickensian character of the twisted or inverted parent.[48] She is not, for instance, a biological mother, instead basing her claim to motherhood on a metaphorically maternal function vis-à-vis her customers. And that function centers, ironically enough, on processes that are antithetical to traditional maternal nurturance insofar as they exploit and degrade her charges, for her preparation and distribution of opium turns her customers' dissipation to her financial advantage.

If we view Princess Puffer as we attempted to view the women in the magazine accounts (that is, as a synecdoche for a feminized Britain), then her version of a maternal impulse might be seen as a metaphor for that larger relationship frequently characterized as parental, Britain's posture toward its colonies. When Disraeli suggested that Victoria take the crown of Empress of India, he was sensitive to the pervasive cultural tendency to idealize motherhood and was aware that the figurehead of a queen who does simultaneous duty as a goddess of the hearth would make the policy of overt British rule of India that much easier for Britons to swallow.[49] Princess Puffer's advertising angle thus recapitulates England's similarly packaged self-presentation as a mother figure concerned with furthering the best interests of her charges. The parallel is reflected in the two names Dickens considered for the character: the one he settled upon, Princess Puffer, plays ironically on the image of a female monarch, and the original name he had chosen for her, Mother Puffer, sardonically emphasizes her supposed maternal attributes.[50] The opium mistress's self-presentation as maternal, apparently only a means to garner more trust and consequently more trade, is thus potentially a scathing commentary on the conflict between the surface presentation and the underlying motives of her national counterpart. Dickens seems to lament that the values often seen as defining the heart of the empire—the domestic ones traditionally associated with femininity—have been crassly commodified.

Princess Puffer's participation in the otherwise male-dominated marketplace might imply an empowerment of women, but it does so only at the expense of any stable definition of femininity. The fact that her particular area of commerce is the traffic in opium smoking also clouds distinctions between Occidental and Oriental, for opium smoking is consistently portrayed elsewhere as the exclusive demesne not only of men but specifically of Oriental men. The Chinese opium master enjoys a monopoly in the opium-smoking market in London because he is supposed to be the sole possessor of the arcane secret of how to prepare the drug for smoking, and smoking unprepared opium is supposed to be at best ineffective, at worst poisonous. As Mother Abdallah notes, "you can't smoke it as you buy it, you see, and Yahee has his own way o' preparin' it, which he won't tell nobody."[51] The narrator of the London Society article elaborates:

> It is this secret which constitutes the rarity of the luxury. To be enjoyed, the opium must be prepared by a competent hand. There are few such in London . . . . How few their number is determined by the fact that when an "opium master" is discovered, even though his den is situate in, without exception, the most vile and villainous part of the metropolis, he is regarded as a person worth visiting by lords and dukes and even princes and kings.[52]

The mysterious exclusivity of the process of preparation gives the opium master an appeal that brings customers from all walks of life to the door of his den. The situation is like a caricature of supply-and-demand economics: consumers are literally addicted to the product, and the supply is uncommonly limited.

But there seems to be something of a chicken-and-egg relationship between the market for opium and the seductive lure of the opium master. If it is true that opium cannot be smoked properly without first dealing with an opium master, then how could someone who has never visited an opium den have a taste for the practice? On the other hand, if customers do not already have that taste, then what brings them to the den in the first place? The answer appears to lie in the exotic appeal of the other world that made the Oriental tale such a popular genre. As the *London Society* reporter sums it up,

> *Of all the carnal delights that over which opium rules as the presiding genius is most shrouded in mystery. It is invested with a weird and fantastic interest (for which its Oriental origin is doubtless in some degree accountable), and there hovers about it a vague fascination, such as is felt towards ghostly legend and the lore of fairy land. There exists a strange yearning to make more intimate acquaintance with the miraculous drug concerning which there is so much whispering, and at the same time a superstitious dread of approaching it, such as, when it comes to the pinch, possesses the rustic believer in the efficacy of repeating a prayer backwards as a means of raising the devil. It is the vulgar supposition that the one occupation of the lives of eastern grandees is to recline on soft cushions and indulge in the charming narcotic; that the thousand and one seductive stories contained in the "Arabian Nights" were composed by writers whose senses were steeped in it.*[53]

The lure of opium smoking for the uninitiated thus has nothing to do with a developed taste for the practice, as of course it cannot have; it is instead due to the appeal of the exotic inherent in this purportedly Oriental luxury, the seductiveness of the radically other that also makes "slumming" such a popular and closely related pastime during the same period. The opium master is smoothly aligned with the consumer marketplace in which products and the public's need for them are manufactured side by side. His exaggerated exclusive control of the opium smoking market in London is part and parcel of the Oriental exoticism that creates that market in the first place.

Even without its caricaturelike extremity, though, the very fact of this Chinese control of the opium market at the heart of the empire would have been disturbing to a British imperial sensibility, for it smacks again of a possible inversion of colonial dynamics—this time of the Indo-Chinese opium trade—and potentially undermines the economic power relations that largely demarcate the center and periphery of the empire. Through the Indo-Chinese opium trade, the English controlled the Chinese largely by means of a similarly exaggerated supply-and-demand scenario in the form of the addiction of thousands of Chinese people to Anglo-Indian opium. But at home in the London market, the Chinese dispense the drug while Britons are the groveling addicts. This Chinese control of Britain would be anxiety-inducing enough even if it were limited to the marginalized population of the East End. But in fact the opium master's influence extends horizontally beyond the East End to more central districts of London and vertically all the way to the uppermost echelons of the empire. Besides attracting "lords and dukes and even princes and kings," one opium master claims to have been visited by no less than the Prince of Wales himself, who allegedly was moved to invite the master and his wife to come directly to the palace to "smokee pipe wi' me."[54] The logical end result, then, is an opium-smoking English population Orientalized from bottom to top.

Princess Puffer demystifies both the Chinese master's mysterious power and his supposedly exclusive control of the opium smoking market as she presides over the arcane ritual whose secret is supposed to be his alone.[55] "Ye'll remember," she exhorts John Jasper, "that nobody but me (and Jack Chinaman t'other side the court; but he can't do it as well as me) has the true secret of mixing it? Ye'll pay up according, deary, won't ye?" (38). Far from allowing the Chinese master unchallenged sway as the high priest of the rites of opium smoking, Princess Puffer even insists that she does his job better than he does, that she has out-Chinese-mastered the Chinese master: "he ain't got the true secret of mixing, though he charges as much as me that has, and more if he can get it" (266). She thus shatters the conventional assumption that the Chinese master has exclusive knowledge, instead gearing her appeal with rhetorical shrewdness toward an audience who wants to believe in superior English know-how with respect to all possible technologies.

This successful proprietorship of an opium den compromises Princess Puffer's identity in terms of both gender and nationality, for she bears the distinctive earmarks traditionally associated with a Chinese man, and her blurred identity necessarily also blurs the identities of the nationalities and genders against which she is unstably contrasted. The instability is evident, for instance, in her theft of a Lascar customer's knife, a charged object that does duty in *Edwin Drood* as an index of Oriental identity, as in one character's categorization of the Oriental patrons of East End opium dens generically as "Chaynermen [and] hother knifers" (277). So when the Lascar reaches for his weapon and finds that "the knife is visible in [Princess Puffer's] dress, not in his" (39), it furthers the implications of her usurpation of the Chinese opium master's role, as she takes on the outward index of Oriental identity. She also implicitly usurps the Lascar's male identity as she displays a surrogate phallus "visible in her dress" while his turns up missing.

This erosion of national and gender identities extends as well to Princess Puffer's relationship with John Jasper, who as we have seen begins to take on her Chineselike physical attributes in the novel's opening scene. But this relationship even goes one step further as it corrodes traditional class distinctions as well. The power imbalance between the princess and her customer initially takes the shape one would expect: the middle-class male Jasper assumes a condescending attitude toward the impoverished woman and her Oriental patrons, dismissing them all as insignificant and "unintelligible." "What visions can *she* have," he muses of his hostess who lies opium-dazed before him, "visions of many butchers' shops, and public-houses, and much credit? Of an increase of hideous customers, and this horrible bedstead set upright again, and this horrible court swept clean? What can she rise to, under any quantity of opium, higher than that!—Eh?" (38). His scoffing betrays an arrogant sense of superiority in terms of both class and gender: because his fellow smoker is a woman he assumes that her highest aspirations would necessarily be in the domestic way of finer furnishings and fancier food, and because she is poor he assumes that she could desire nothing more than an increase of food, money, basic physical comforts, and alcohol. But his complacency proves frighteningly unfounded when turned tables reveal that her chief aspiration has in fact been to have power over him, a goal she appears by then to have attained: "I heard ye say once, when I was lying where you're lying, and you were making your speculation upon me, 'Unintelligible!' I heard you say so, of two more than me [the Chinese and Lascar customers]. But don't ye be too sure always; don't ye be too sure, beauty! . . . Practice makes perfect. I may have learned the secret how to make ye talk, my deary" (271–72). By this point in the novel Princess Puffer (and presumably the reader) strongly suspects that Jasper harbors the secret of having murdered his nephew, Edwin Drood. To make him talk would thus be to gain a blackmailer's advantage over him, more than reversing the hierarchy he so smugly presupposes. As Princess Puffer recalls aloud the long-ago days when Jasper was "quite new" to opium smoking and the later time when he "was able by-and-bye to take [his] pipes with the best of 'em" (268), it becomes apparent that "practice makes perfect" indeed, and that she has gradually gained power over this Englishman through the will- and character-usurping influence of opium.[56] And that insidious influence has enabled her to overturn the local gender-, class-race-, and nationality-based power relations, now casting this middle-class Englishman in a subservient role and placing the poor woman and her Oriental comrades in a position of dominance. The atmosphere in the opium den, then, ultimately corrodes all boundaries that give shape to social identities—between male and female, pure and contaminated, upper- and lower-class, household and marketplace, domestic and foreign, English and Oriental.

VI

"It Begins with the Chinese, but Does Not End with Them"

Opium Smoking and the Orientalized Domestic Scene in England

ALTHOUGH *The Mystery of Edwin Drood* was left only half finished at Dickens's death, the portion that remains nonetheless offers a more three-dimensional image of the opium den than the preceding magazine articles do, for Dickens's opium den appears within a larger, more diversified narrative, thus providing points of reference outside the opium den but still within the same unit of discourse. Princess Puffer, for instance, is only one of several women who appear in the novel, and the opium den over which she presides includes a significant element that is missing from the magazine narratives: an opium-smoking English*man*. As we have seen, these added details serve as points of triangulation for a more textured perspective on the relationships between British identity, gender, and opium smoking. But the longer, more varied narrative of *Edwin Drood* also projects a similarly detailed idea of the Orient, and the development of all of these terms in the English cathedral town of Cloisterham as well as the opium den at the East End of London opens up a perspective on another factor that was implicit in the opium den narratives that preceded *Edwin Drood* and becomes increasingly important in those that follow: the relationships between opium smoking and the English domestic scene.

The complication of gender and class identities we have seen in *Edwin Drood* also complicates any available notion of the domestic environment, for insofar as the ideal Victorian middle-class domestic scene has at center stage a virtuous and maternal feminine figure, the reconfiguration of notions of femininity also necessarily alters the rest of the scene. Although any argument about the domestic scene's ultimate shape after its reconfiguration in *Edwin Drood* must resort to speculation about the novel's incomplete plot, one can nonetheless see the progress of the process in such available details as Princess Puffer's commercialized distortion of the maternal ideal and her influence over John Jasper, who carries the effects of her opium den's atmosphere back to his middle-class home in a provincial cathedral town. In this and other instances, *Edwin Drood* explores the insidious influence of the opium den and other things Oriental on environments outside of the opium den, outside of the East End, and outside of London, but still within England. Dickens shows the Oriental atmosphere seeping out of the East End den and into the homes and daily lives of middle-class Britons who may never have had firsthand experience of opium smoke, a crossover that becomes a focus of subsequent opium den narratives such as those written by Oscar Wilde and Arthur Conan Doyle at the end of the century.[1]

"How Can That Be Here!": The Mystery of Edwin Drood

This dissolution of the supposed boundary between a familiar British domestic environment and an exotic Orient is apparent immediately in *Edwin Drood*'s opening paragraph, which consists of John Jasper's impressions of his opium-inspired visions:

(37)

> *An ancient English Cathedral town? How can the ancient English Cathedral town be here! The well-known massive grey square tower of its old Cathedral? How can that be here! There is no spike of rusty iron in the air, between the eye and it, from any point of the real prospect. What is the spike that intervenes, and who has set it up? Maybe it is set up by the Sultan's orders for the impaling of a horde of Turkish robbers, one by one. It is so, for cymbals clash, and the Sultan goes by to his palace in long procession. Ten thousand scimitars flash in the sunlight.*[2]

The reader can know neither the setting of the scene nor whose impression of it is being presented until near the end of the second paragraph. All that is available in this opening tableau is the venerable English cathedral town in the background, the vast procession of scimitar-wielding Orientals in the foreground, the rusty iron spike on which they are supposed to impale hordes of their enemies in the middle distance, and the speaker's emphatic sense that these elements do not belong together in the present setting.

This fantastic mixing of the English cathedral town and the Orient becomes a theme for the novel as a whole, and as the narrator soon lets on, it is in this instance a direct result of opium smoking, for subsequent paragraphs show that the corporeal setting of these airy visions is an East London opium den. The physical presence of the den in the first paragraph is evident only in the rusty spike that turns out to be a post of the den's broken-down bedstead, but its influence is pervasive. It is significant, for instance, that this spike forms the visual transition between the Oriental horde and the English cathedral in

Jasper's vision, for it thus suggests that it is the environment of the opium den that punctures the boundary between the familiar British scene and the exotic and violent Orient, allowing one infectiously to enter the open wound in the other.

Jasper leaves the den and returns to the cathedral town to resume his daylight existence as one of the last things one might expect a patron of an opium den to be, the cathedral's choirmaster. But he seems to trail the den's corrosive atmosphere behind him as the division between his private London life and his public Cloisterham one dissolves to the extent that he even smokes opium in his own bedroom in his provincial home (77). And, like Princess Puffer in her den, Jasper passes his contagion to other individuals in his hometown as he actively drums up new recruits for opium. He seems to slip some into a "stirrup cup" he serves to two guests, for instance, as his sly, secretive attitude while preparing it suggests: "Jasper looks observantly from one to the other, slightly smiles, and turns his back to mix a jug of mulled wine at the fire. It seems to require much mixing and compounding" (100), and one of the guests later reports that "it overcame me in the strangest and most sudden manner" (103).[3] Jasper apparently repeats the ruse when he shares a bottle of liquor with the gravedigger Durdles: after the seasoned alcoholic Durdles is knocked out by the drink, Jasper coyly notes to himself that "I have suspicions that my bottle was filled with something stiffer than either of us supposed" (158). We are thus presented with a picture of an outwardly conformist middle-class citizen who unexpectedly leads a subversive hidden life centered around and enabled by the influence of opium. And this hidden life is not safely confined to the distant East End opium den. It instead is only fueled there and then comes back to a middle-class home in a quaint English village to catalyze the synthesis of the British domestic environment and the Orient. Like xenophobic cold war fantasies of the 1950s United States, such as *Invasion of the Body Snatchers* and *Invaders from Mars*, *Edwin Drood* draws a scenario in which an insidious foreign influence has already infected the seemingly upright citizen next door and is working its way outward from the landing site into the fundamental fabric of the invaded culture.

The swarms of threatening Orientals in Jasper's vision would have been especially resonant for Dickens and his readers, for at the time he was writing *Edwin Drood,* Britons were still reeling from the sensationalistic tales of Oriental savagery that followed the infamous Indian Mutiny of 1857. Narratives of the revolt that returned to and emerged from England were particularly horrifying (and fascinating) to the English, for as they luridly portrayed it, the Indian soldiers not only failed to protect British subjects but actually attacked them, supposedly torturing and killing hundreds of civilian women and children.[4] Dickens himself was extravagantly resentful of what he called the "Oriental race" in India and viewed it as a threat that needed to be eradicated. In a letter to Angela Burdett-Coutts written immediately after the Mutiny, his righteous indignation swelled even to genocidal· fury as he argued that the obligation of the "Commander in Chief in India" was to "do [his] utmost to exterminate the Race upon whom the stain of late cruelties rested, . . . to blot it out of mankind and raze it off the face of the Earth."[5]

This particular version of the violent Orient is mirrored in *Edwin Drood* by the character of Neville Landless, a young orphan from Ceylon who has come to Cloisterham to study with its Minor Canon Crisparkle. Neville voices the sentiments popularly attributed to the repressed sepoys as he recounts the effects of a youth spent in subjection to a "cruel brute" of a stepfather in Ceylon:

(90)

> *I have had, sir, from my earliest remembrance, to suppress a deadly and bitter hatred. This has made me secret and revengeful. I have been always tyrannically held down by the strong hand. This has driven me, in my weakness, to the resource of being false and mean. I have been stinted of education, liberty, money, dress, the very necessaries of life, the commonest pleasures of childhood, the commonest possessions of youth. This has caused me to be utterly wanting in I don't know what emotions, or remembrances, or good instincts.*

The terms in which Neville describes himself trace the outlines of the classic demonic Oriental ("secret and revengeful," "false and mean," "utterly wanting in . . . good instincts"),[6] and the narrator shades them in as he adds more terms from the litany of Oriental stereotypes (dark, cagey, predatory, catlike). To him Neville and his twin sister Helena are

(84–85)

> *an unusually handsome lithe young fellow, and an unusually handsome lithe girl; much alike; both very dark, and very rich in color; she almost of the gipsy type; something untamed about them both; a certain air upon them of hunter and huntress; yet withal a certain air of being the objects of the chase, rather than the followers. Slender, supple, quick of eye and limb; half shy, half defiant; fierce of look; an indefinable kind of pause coming and going on their whole expression, both of face and form, which might be equally likened to the pause before a crouch, or a bound.*

The manifestation of this catlike Oriental nature in Neville (more about Helena in a moment) is particularly charged.[7] In conjunction with his history of being "tyrannically held down by the strong hand," his stereotypical Oriental nature suggests that, like the Chinese in London after the opium wars, perhaps he is in England to carry out a "secret and revengeful" mission against India's parallel tyrannical stepparent, England. The cliché also suggests again the idea of a contagious Oriental identity capable of diluting or even superseding the British one as it apparently has in Neville's case: as he says, "I have been brought up among abject and servile dependents of an inferior race, and may easily have contracted some affinity with them. Sometimes, I don't know but that it may be a drop of what is tigerish in their blood" (90).[8] Although Neville dresses in English style, seeks an English education, and in general refuses to view himself as a native of Ceylon, his nationality and/or race are ultimately unclear. The reader knows only that his mother died in Ceylon when he was a child and that he was raised by his stepfather (88). Like *The Moonstone's* Ezra Jennings, he is ultimately neither English nor Oriental but a hybrid of the two, and thus is left "landless."

This instance of an Oriental admixture in the English cathedral town is not linked directly to the contagion from the opium den that Jasper has been bringing back, and seems to illustrate at a more generalized level the auctioneer Mr. Sapsea's boast that "if I have not gone to foreign countries, young man, foreign countries have come to me." Sapsea's scenario seems especially true of the Orient, for the evidence with which he supports his assertion consists of "cups and saucers of Chinese make" and "bamboo and sandal-wood from the East Indies," and "it is the same with Japan, with Egypt" (64). Sapsea sketches a quasi-Coleridgean sense of colonial commerce as cultural leakage, viewing products from the Orient as incursions of the countries themselves onto English soil, though he has none of Coleridge's sense of foreboding and indeed even revels in the appearance of foreign countries on his doorstep. But the rest of the novel is not always so complacent, for this contagion through commodities also lurks immediately below the surface elsewhere in the text, most obviously in the form of opium but also in various threats to the character who seems most to represent pure British femininity, Rosa Bud, or Rosebud.

If Princess Puffer represents a compromised version of British femininity, then the model of purity against whom she is contrasted is Rosebud, who as the novel opens is about to become a bride, to bloom into the domestic angel. But Rosebud's pure British femininity is under constant threat of being alloyed with various versions of the Orient. It comes to her doorstep just as it does to Sapsea's in the form of foreign commodities when, for instance, she insists on being taken "to the Lumps-of-Delight shop" where she indulges "with great zest" a passion for the "Turkish sweetmeat" (58). She thus takes the Orient into her body (à la Coleridge) and does so with a sensuality that brings submerged sexual connotations of the act closer to the surface as she goes about eating by "taking off and rolling up a pair of little pink gloves like rose-leaves, and occasionally putting her little pink fingers to her rosy lips, to cleanse them from the Dust of Delight that comes off the Lumps" (58).

Even marriage, conventionally the Victorian woman's apotheosis as the entry into her proper domestic sphere, is associated in Rosebud's case with the threat of Orientalization. First she seems destined to be sucked into the source itself as her fiancé, Edwin, threatens her with "being carried off to Egypt," where he plans to further the goals of empire as an engineer. Rosebud cannot imagine that a proper English girl could do other than "hate Arabs, and Turks, and Fellahs, and people . . . At least, she *must* hate the Pyramids," and she views her impending fate with dread (59). Although she is ultimately freed from her would-be colonial destiny when her engagement to Edwin is broken, the threat of a sexual alliance with the Orient nonetheless persists in other forms, for she is the object of the amorous attentions of the novel's two ambiguous, suggestively Oriental men. During his short time in town, the Anglo-Indian Neville Landless has fallen in love with Rosebud, prompting the nagging spectre of miscegenation once again to rear its head. This particular threat is apparently averted, for in the finished portion of the novel it never reaches beyond Neville's expressions of admiration, which prompt a violent quarrel with Edwin. But an even more threatening mirror of Neville's desire is presented in the form of the strange sexual threat of the Orientalesque John Jasper, who is described as "a dark man . . . with thick, lustrous, well-arranged black hair and whisker" (43), highly charged physical attributes in this narrative in which dark "un-English" complexions have already been linked with insidious Orientalism. Several critics have even argued that Jasper would ultimately have been exposed as an undercover Oriental agent who had secretly come to England to execute various violent designs.[9]

But whatever the finished novel would have shown, it is clear from what Dickens did complete that Jasper conspicuously fits the stereotype of the dark and smolderingly violent Oriental developed elsewhere in the narrative. And, in addition to his contraction of the Oriental contagion of the opium den in the novel's opening scene, Jasper also resembles the Chinese opium masters of the magazine articles with his vampirelike hypnotic charisma that exercises a dreaded hold upon Englishwomen. Rosebud, who is Jasper's music pupil, describes this almost supernatural influence: "He has made a slave of me with his looks. He has forced me to understand him, without his saying a word; and he has forced me to keep silence, without his uttering a threat" (95). He is most menacing, she says, "when a glaze comes over [his eyes] (which is sometimes the case), and he seems to wander away into a frightful sort of dream in which he threatens most . . . [and is] more terrible to me than ever" (95). In other words, Jasper is most powerful when he has been fortified by opium, for Rosebud's description of his glazed expression matches the "strange film come over your eyes" that Edwin observes earlier and Jasper brushes aside with the explanation that "I have been taking opium" (47). (The association recurs when Edwin meets Princess Puffer in the street wearing a "strange blind stare" [177]; "'Good Heaven!' he thinks, . . . 'Like Jack that night!'" and she answers yes when he asks, "Do you eat opium?" [178]). Like the strange charisma of the opium masters, Jasper's influence is also contagious. When he corners Rosebud in a garden and "stands leaning against the sundial—setting, as it were, his black mark upon the very face of day" (228), his dark contamination lingers over the sundial even after he has gone, "as though he had invested it with some awful quality from his own nature" (234). Whereas the Orientalizing influence of opium in the den has only been shown extending to people, its powers are apparently enhanced when an Englishman carries it out into the light of day, for it now extends even to inanimate objects (a phenomenon that will be explored in greater depth by Wilde and Conan Doyle) and is able to overpower an Englishwoman without ever bringing her into contact with its smoke.

It seems as if Rosebud would have been saved from a union with either of these quasi-Oriental men had the novel been finished, for there are strong hints that she was instead to be paired with the retired sailor who becomes her protector in London. But even that would be at best an equivocal rescue, for this seaman is only tenuously tied to England (or any other land, for that matter), even taking pains to recreate in his lodgings the atmosphere of a ship at sea, and he is implicitly linked to a violent Orient through his name of Tartar, "a name as redolent of the East as a whiff of hashish," as one critic has put it.[10] There seems to be no example in *Edwin Drood* of British identity that is unalloyed with the Orient, and no place where the ubiquitous and insidious Oriental contagion does not pose a threat to British femininity.

But if there is no unalloyed British identity, then surely there can be no unequivocal British femininity. In fact Dickens goes one better: there is no stable version of femininity at all. Although the opening scene of *Edwin Drood* initially follows the magazine narratives' conventional portrayal of women as implicitly weaker in both physical and moral terms and more likely to succumb to the Oriental infection than men, that implication does not follow through even to the conclusion of the scene, for Princess Puffer's contagion immediately overpowers her Englishman customer, and later she remains in control when he is stupefied by opium. Ultimately, the strongest and most disciplined character in the novel is also a woman, Neville's twin sister, Helena Landless. Her brother pays tribute to her staunchness, claiming that "nothing in our misery ever subdued her, though it often cowed me" (90), and even the bigoted townspeople of Cloisterham who are quick to suspect Neville of murder nonetheless respectfully acknowledge his sister's will as strong enough for both of them, believing that "but for his poor sister . . . he would be in the daily commission

of murder" (198). In fact her resolve is so strong that it is an intimidating, potentially destructive power in its own right. This is most evident in contrast to
Rosebud, who says to Helena, "you are so womanly and handsome. You seem
to have resolution and power enough to crush me. I shrink into nothing by the
side of your presence even" (94). Helena thus merges attributes traditionally
separated along gender lines, appearing to be the essence of what is "womanly
and handsome" but also possessing "resolution and power enough to crush."
This superhuman resolve has compromised her femininity since her early days,
for Neville relates that it was she who planned their several childhood escape
attempts, and "each time she dressed as a boy, and showed the daring of a man"
(90). Her strong will's capacity to make Rosebud "shrink into nothing by the
side of [her] presence" suggests that this ambiguous gender, nationality, and race
that she embodies will supersede and even eradicate their British counterparts.

"An Echo of Someone Else's Music":
The Picture of Dorian Gray

Once *The Mystery of Edwin Drood* brought opium dens into a broad popular
consciousness, representations of them proliferated. Like the generations of explorers who traveled to the East to seek the Orient they knew only through
imaginative literature, Dickens's fans set out for London's East End searching
for the actual setting of *Edwin Drood* and hoping to experience firsthand the
ambience they had found so compelling in the novel. Thus was born a new
generation of quasi-journalistic opium den accounts with increasingly codified
conventions.[11] This growing interest in entering popular fiction's version of the
opium den is accompanied by an increasing tendency for the observers to fic-
tionally create themselves in their visits to the East End, as the generation of
slummers after Dickens delights in dressing up in East End costume to carry
out its increasingly imaginative expeditions. Their reports thus echo imperialist
exploration narratives such as Sir Richard Burton's *A Pilgrimage to El-Medinah
and Mecca* and Charles Doughty's *Travels in Arabia Deserta,* which, as Daniel
Bivona says, "reveal their authors' almost 'childish' delight in exploration, disguise, and the penetration of mysteries that lurk behind the veil of cultural
boundaries."[12] But as these expeditions become more distanced from the world
of the observer on one level (he takes on an alternative identity, leaving his daily
personality outside the East End), they become less distanced on another, for
the explorers who follow Dickens into the opium den are no longer merely
observers; they instead assume new identities that presumably harmonize with
the environment they inhabit and more boldly partake of the opium smoke
itself.[13]

   While Dickens's influence loomed large in journalistic accounts of opium dens, it was even more pervasive in explicitly fictional narratives. John Jasper is the prototype of a character who became the object of a consistent fascination for Victorian fiction writers: the respectable middle-class man who leads a second, hidden life of uninhibited self-indulgence in London's East End, a character seen also in such other fictions as Stevenson's *The Strange Case of Dr. Jekyll and Mr. Hyde* (1886). *Edwin Drood* is also the first example of a subgenre of the double-life tale in which the protagonist's shift between identities is associated specifically with opium dens and Oriental ambience. Later examples include Oscar Wilde's *The Picture of Dorian Gray* and Arthur Conan Doyle's Sherlock Holmes adventure "The Man With the Twisted Lip" (both 1891), which draw into question divisions between British and Oriental and between the imagined poles of the decadent East End and the morally sound suburbs.

Like John Jasper, Wilde's Dorian Gray appears to be an upstanding citizen while he secretly leads a second life that flouts conventional middle-class morality, and he reaches the depths of his decadence amidst "the heavy odour of opium" in an East End den. But unlike Jasper, Dorian's first exposure to the drug is in a London residence rather than an East End den as he breathes "the thin blue wreaths of smoke that [curl] up in such fanciful whorls from [the] heavy opium-tainted cigarette" of his bohemian aristocrat mentor, Lord Henry Wotton (24).[14] Wilde thus takes a step beyond the opium-associated blending of the Orient and the domestic scene portrayed by Dickens, for opium in *Dorian Gray* seems at home in a domestic environment where it initially has no apparent connection to either the Orient or the East End.

Conversely, when Oriental elements first appear in *Dorian Gray,* they have no immediate connection to opium. We first see the Orient incorporated into Dorian's daily existence with his domestic decor that emulates Lord Henry's "long-fringed Persian rugs" and "large blue china jars" (69). Like *Edwin Drood's* Sapsea, Dorian delights in surrounding himself with Oriental commodities, but with none of Sapsea's overt awareness of cultural crossover and with an amplified interest that might be called obsession. In fact Dorian's exotic objets d'art function as something like addictive substances themselves. In the scene leading up to his opium den visit Dorian becomes transfixed by a cabinet at the other end of his library, "as though it were a thing that could fascinate and make afraid, as though it held something that he longed for and yet almost loathed." As "a mad craving [comes] over him," he unlocks the cabinet and opens a secret drawer from which he takes "a small Chinese box of black and gold-dust lacquer, elaborately wrought, the sides patterned with curved waves, and the silken cords hung with round crystals and tasselled inplaited metal threads. He open[s] it. Inside [is] a green paste, waxy in lustre, the odour curiously heavy and persistent." He hesitates for a moment, smiling enigmatically and shivering over the box and its mysterious contents until he finally dresses "commonly," hails a cab, and orders the cabman to drive "towards the river" (that is, to the East End dock district), where he visits an opium den (218–19). The waxy green paste is of course opium,[15] which now resides in a gentleman's library and is associated with an alteration of his identity (like the slummers in other narratives, he disguises himself as an East Ender by dressing "commonly") and with an irresistible urge to go out and play in the East End. It may be either the waxy paste or the box containing it that has these effects on Dorian, but either way, Wilde clouds the direction of the flow of Oriental influence between the opium den and the middle-class home, a flow that was represented implicitly as unidirectional in *Edwin Drood*. Whereas John Jasper initially appeared smoking opium in an East End den and was later seen using the drug at home, Dorian's situation is exactly inverted, and his opium den debauch is actually an extension of an episode begun in his home.

Wilde does not portray the flow of Oriental influence as fully inverted, however, for although the East End den is not necessarily the source of Oriental elements in *Dorian Gray,* it predictably serves as their focus, as the smoky atmosphere of the den proves once again to be the natural habitat of grotesque and animalistic Orientals, such as "some Malays . . . crouching by a little charcoal stove playing with bone counters, and showing their white teeth as they chattered" (223). But this is not to say that the den embodies an authoritative, stable version of Orientalness, for once again its denizens seem to be neither English nor Oriental but a mixture of the two, such as an otherwise apparently English prostitute who sports "a crooked smile, like a Malay crease" and "a half-caste, in a ragged turban and a shabby ulster" (224–25). The half-caste's turban and ulster seem to be indexes of conflicting but simultaneous Oriental and British components of his identity. But it is significant that an ulster is not just generally British; it is specifically Irish and thus invokes another group besides Orientals that has been disenfranchised by the British Empire. The national-racial aspects of the opium den habitués' identities accrete and multiply to form a picture of the den as the arena of a generalized return of the repressed, a space in which the Empire's disempowered come to exercise influence over the supposedly powerful upper-middle-class Englishmen who are gradually drained of their identities.

It is thus tempting to read Wilde's opium den and *The Picture of Dorian Gray* in general as a veiled commentary on British imperialism, a reading indirectly supported by the novel's prominent concern with "influence." "To influence a person," says Lord Henry, "is to give him one's own soul. . . . He becomes an echo of someone else's music, an actor of a part that has not been written for him" (40–41). Much as Coleridge's anti-imperialist "Fears in Solitude" lamented that the British had "borne to distant tribes slavery and pangs, / And, deadlier far, our vices," so does Lord Henry regret that, once a person has been influenced, "His sins, if there are such things as sins, are borrowed" (41). Read in this light, *The Picture of Dorian Gray* could emerge as yet another tale of a turning of the tables of British imperialism, for Dorian's "sins that are new" cluster around the smoking of opium, and if "his sins are borrowed," then they are borrowed from the East End and the Orient. If he "becomes an echo of someone else's music, an actor of a part that has not been written for him," then the composers and playwrights are the former singers and actors, and the Englishman who used to be among the puppetmasters is now among the puppets. The opium den would thus appear once again as a foothold for a hostile invasion by repressed colonial peoples (especially Orientals), the catalyst for a gradual usurpation of British identity by means of an insidious reversal of the identity-eroding process of influence.

But the text will not ultimately allow such a convenient reading, for a reversal of roles requires two stable roles to begin with, a criterion *Dorian Gray* conspicuously fails to meet. The half-caste, for instance, is not easily categorized as either an Orientalized Briton or an Anglicized Oriental. Rather, like all the other inhabitants of this den, he does not resolve into any coherent identity. Orientalization is only a subset of the opium den's more general tendency toward the dilution of *all* kinds of identity, and the Oriental identity is no more stable than any other. Patrons of the den are not simply Orientalized; more accurately they are drained of race, class, gender, even humanity as they dissociate into isolated features of vaguely human forms: "the grotesque things that lay in such fantastic postures on the ragged mattresses. The twisted limbs, the gaping mouths, the staring lustreless eyes" (224). And the proprietors' identities are no more coherent: they are neither Oriental nor English nor Irish nor any other recognizable nationality or race. Instead they are themselves "grotesque things" perhaps best represented by "the squat misshapen figure" who serves as doorkeeper, a deformed, indeterminate personage who represents the logical extent of at least one strain of widespread anxieties about miscegenation and cultural blending.[16]

"A Sort of Eastern Divan": "The Man With the Twisted Lip"

The character of the middle-class Englishman who leads a second, secret life to which he passes through an East End opium den is picked up and elaborated a few months after the first book publication of *The Picture of Dorian Gray* in Arthur Conan Doyle's Sherlock Holmes adventure "The Man With the Twisted Lip."[17] Like *Dorian Gray*, Conan Doyle's tale also portrays Oriental influence extending well beyond the East End den into British domestic scenes, where it problematizes various notions of identity. The double identity of the middle-class man explodes into a surprising duplicity of all the trappings of middle-class existence, including home, occupation, income, even domestic decor. Everything that seems middle-class and British in this tale also turns out to have an Oriental and/or lower-class identity barely hidden beneath its surface, and the slippery, too-permeable boundary between these pairs of identities once again appears—at least at first glance—to be the East End opium den.

The adventure is initiated by a disruption of domestic order as Watson is torn away from his easy chair beside his wife and her needlework to answer another young wife's request that he retrieve her husband from an opium den and restore him to his empty hearthside. The good doctor journeys to what Holmes later calls "the vilest murder-trap on the whole river-side," an East End opium den run by a "rascally Lascar" and a "sallow Malay" (624–26),[18] and coincidentally finds Holmes there investigating the disappearance of yet another young husband who was last seen peering from a window upstairs. Immediately the den exerts a consistent and corrosive influence over the distant domestic scene, drawing three middle-class husbands from their homes, leaving fretting wives next to empty easy chairs.

And once these men are drawn from their homes into the opium den, they follow previous East End expeditionaries in assuming second identities supposedly consistent with their haunts. The man for whom Watson searches becomes quasi-Oriental, "with yellow, pasty face, drooping lids and pin-point pupils" (623), and Holmes is at first unrecognizable in his disguise as a seasoned opium smoker, "very thin, very wrinkled, . . . an opium pipe dangling down from between his knees" (625). Holmes ultimately discovers that the man for whom he has been searching has also been leading two lives with the opium den as gateway between them, spending his weekdays ironically earning a fortune as a beggar in the city and his evenings and weekends as a husband and father in the suburbs, using a rented room in the opium den to change from suburban family man to beggar and back again.

The opium den thus serves as the gateway between the two poles of Neville St. Clair's double life, and it seems at first as if the den is a closeable valve between the two existences, opening twice a day to allow only the beggar into the City and only the suburban family man out of it. But it becomes increasingly evident that assorted detritus accompanies the man in each of his passages until the two existences are indistinguishable from one another. Most obviously, the St. Clair family's suburban lifestyle is ironically financed by Neville's begging. But the two realms mesh in other, more subtle ways as well.

When the police search for the missing St. Clair, for instance, the secret of his dual identity is nearly given away by an expensive suit of clothes and some children's building bricks in the beggar's room above the opium den. Thus elements of St. Clair's two existences mix with one another until it is impossible to say whether he is a family man impersonating a beggar or a beggar posing as a family man.

At first glance, it appears as if class is more the contagious factor than Orientalism—St. Clair becomes a beggar rather than an Oriental, after all— and that the Orient is more or less safely contained in the vile murder trap on the riverside.[19] But a closer look reveals that the Orient is initially unapparent outside the den only because it has so fully integrated with what at first seems to be unexceptionably British. In the story's first paragraph, Watson describes Isa Whitney (the man he retrieves from the den), "brother of the late Elias Whitney, D.D., Principal of the Theological College of St. George's." Whitney initially appears to be quintessentially respectable English middle-class, but Watson immediately appends to his credentials the observation that he is "much addicted to opium" and has even grown to resemble the Oriental smokers in previous accounts, "with yellow, pasty face, drooping lids and pin-point pupils" (623).[20] Watson implies that this habit responsible for reducing the otherwise promising Whitney to "the wreck and ruin of a noble man" has an English rather than an Oriental source, for it ostensibly originates in De Quincey: "The habit grew upon him . . . from some foolish freak when he was at college, for having read De Quincey's description of his dreams and sensations, he had drenched his tobacco with laudanum" (623). But even this tenuous Englishness drops away, for apart from the fact that De Quincey himself associated his own habit with fundamentally Oriental rather than British practices, he also never smoked opium but instead only drank it in the form of laudanum. The smoking of opium was an exotic Oriental practice essentially unheard of in England in De Quincey's time and was thought of as a peculiarly Oriental vice even in Dickens's day. The fact that Whitney's habit was acquired not from a bamboo pipe in an East End den but rather from a regular British brier or meerschaum smoked in rooms at Oxbridge suggests that the Britishness and Orientalness of the habit have become inseparable, that what was peculiarly Oriental is now unexceptionably British, and vice versa.[21]

If Whitney's smoking of laudanum-laced tobacco suggests that British and Oriental are not differentiable, Holmes's peculiar tobacco-smoking practices insist that they are merged. Watson describes the great detective's ritual as he prepares to spend the night in a guest bedroom in the St. Clairs' home in a London suburb:

(633)

He . . . wandered about the room collecting pillows from his bed, and cushions from the sofa and armchairs. With these he constructed a sort of Eastern divan, upon which he perched himself cross-legged, with an ounce of shag tobacco and a box of matches laid out in front of him. In the dim light of the lamp I saw him sitting there, an old brier pipe between his lips, his eyes fixed vacantly upon the corner of the ceiling, the blue smoke curling up from him, silent, motionless, with the light shining upon his strong set aquiline features.

Holmes's tobacco-smoking posture echoes that of the by now familiar Oriental opium smoker but with a strange amalgam of incongruous British domestic elements. He sits on an "Eastern divan," but it is composed of armchair and sofa cushions. With "pipe between his lips, his eyes fixed vacantly upon the corner of the ceiling, the blue smoke curling up from him, silent, motionless," he resembles the Orientals in the opium dens, but he nonetheless still has a stolidly Occidental countenance "with the light shining upon his strong set aquiline features." The room "full of a dense tobacco haze" looks much like the "room, thick and heavy with the brown opium smoke" Watson described in the East End den (624), but this room is a bedchamber in a suburban villa, and the smoke is from English shag tobacco rather than opium.

Although anti-opium enthusiasts like Rev. George Piercy attributed the supposedly growing Oriental contagion to English patronage of the opium dens of London's East End, "The Man With the Twisted Lip" gradually takes that assumption apart. At the beginning, we find Isa Whitney smoking opium from an English tobacco pipe at an English university; in the midst of the adventure, we see St. Clair's passage through the opium den apparently blending the East End with the suburban domestic scene even though he never smokes opium; and by the end of the story, an incipient Oriental nature is discernible in British domestic elements that are disconnected in any direct physical sense from either opium, the East End, or the Orient. Objects and practices are simultaneously characteristic of both the opium den and the British domestic scene as the sofa cushions are also an Eastern divan, the shag tobacco plays the role of opium, and the suburban bedroom doubles as an opium den.

This Oriental presence in the nineteenth-century British domestic environment has much in common with late twentieth-century theories about viral diseases. Unlike bacterial infections, which besiege the body for a time and either kill it or are killed themselves, current orthodoxy has it that viruses enter the cells of the organism, sometimes even becoming a part of its very genetic structure. The viruses thus invisibly reproduce themselves with each reproduction of the host cell, of which they are now a permanent part, and may go on replicating and integrating with the host cells for years without manifesting noticeable symptoms only to cause unpredictable complications in the later life of the organism.[22] A similar process seems to be at work in Conan Doyle's undifferentiable Anglo-Oriental domestic scene, in which Oriental elements enter British culture via the opium den or other avenues and then become permanent but almost invisible components of the culture, integrating and reproducing with the host culture only to cause unexpected complications later on.[23] Just as the opium smoke enters the smoker's body, permanently altering the cells and restructuring the smoker's identity,[24] so do foreign elements introduced into a culture become part of that culture, restructuring the national identity until what were previously perceived as rigidly divided cultures are now inseparable.

This cultural blending is both enticing and frightening to nineteenth-century Britons—enticing perhaps because it brings the often romanticized, adventurous frontiers of colonialism to one's doorstep, but frightening because those frontiers themselves are often threatening. Bringing them home gives a presumably hostile culture a foothold, perhaps ultimately enabling the replacement of a national identity which at least *seemed* predictable with an unpredictable changeling. The late nineteenth century's wariness of the opium den, then, is inseparable from simultaneous anxieties about the imperial process. Britons at the end of the century felt a growing awareness that the British Empire could no longer be viewed as an entity in which the home culture of England simply overwrote the Oriental culture of the colonies, nor could "British culture" or even "British identity" be taken for granted as stable, objective essences. Instead, they began to realize, the British Empire must be viewed as an unpredictable multinational entity at every level from nation to individual and from the outposts in the colonies to the hearthsides in London.

Notes

Works Cited

Index

Notes

Introduction

1. I put "drugs" within quotes because of the many questions the usages of the term beg. What, for instance, differentiates drugs from nondrugs? One need look no further than the historically uneven application of the term to, say, opium and alcohol to see the degree to which the categories are defined culturally.
2. Schneider, *Coleridge, Opium and Kubla Khan*, 49.
3. Hayter, *Opium and the Romantic Imagination*, 12.
4. Representative of this moralizing impulse is the following assertion: "No conclusions can be drawn from the mental processes of such men as Coleridge and De Quincey, exceptional in any age and living in a psychological environment now utterly vanished, which will be valid for the defiant ignorant adolescents who are the great majority of today's drug addicts" (Hayter, *Opium and the Romantic Imagination*, 12).
5. "His predicament was not simply a matter of sapped will," says Lefebure; "his intellectual capacity was fearfully eroded: his sense of truth hopelessly distorted (one of the major effects of morphine addiction). The present study is an attempt to present Samuel Taylor Coleridge as it seems he really was—a junkie" (Lefebure, *Samuel Taylor Coleridge*, 14).
6. Also worth mentioning in an overview of previous work on opium in nineteenth-century England are Terry M. Parssinen's *Secret Passions, Secret Remedies: Narcotic Drugs in British Society, 1820–1930* (1983) and *Flowers in the Blood: The Story of Opium* (1981) by Dean Latimer and Jeff Goldberg. Parssinen's book, while often brief in its presentation and interpretation of evidence, is nonetheless a valuable source of information. Latimer and Goldberg's book, which bears the entertainingly quirky stamp of the pro-drug-culture magazine *High Times* of which both authors were editors, unearths some interesting tidbits other treatments miss.
7. Brantlinger, *Rule of Darkness*, 11, 88. A similar position is elaborated in terms of race, nationality, and gender by Gayatri Chakravorty Spivak, who argues that "both as object of colonialist historiography and as subject of insurgency, the ideological construction of gender keeps the male dominant. If, in the context of colonial production, the subaltern has no history and cannot speak, the subaltern as female is even more deeply in shadow" (Spivak, "Can the Subaltern Speak?" 287).
8. The effect to which I refer here is similar to what Homi K. Bhabha calls "hybridity": "a *problematic* of colonial representation and individuation that reverses the effects of the colonialist disavowal, so that other 'denied' knowledges enter upon the dominant discourse and estrange the basis of its authority—its rules of recognition. . . .

What is irremediably estranging in the presence of the hybrid . . . is that the difference of cultures can no longer be identified or evaluated as objects of epistemologi-
cal or moral contemplation: they are not simply *there* to be seen or appropriated"
(Bhabha, "Signs Taken for Wonders," 175).

9. Spivak, "Can the Subaltern Speak?" 292. One representative example of the move
she warns against is Eric Meyer's exhortation to read "the narrative(s) of Romantic
Orientalism through the eye of the Eastern other who is constituted as the obscure
object of Western desire" (Meyer, "I Know Thee Not," 685). By presuming the
protean ability unproblematically to occupy the perspective of "the Eastern other,"
Meyer enacts a version of the very stance he deplores, "the panoptic positioning
of a presumed 'omniscient' narrator who asserts control over the multiple internal
fracturings of that field" (Ibid., 682).

10. Kabbani, *Europe's Myths of Orient*, 6.

11. Said, *Orientalism*, 7, 9, 204.

12. Clifford, *The Predicament of Culture*, 262, 259.

13. Lowe, *Critical Terrains*, 7.

14. See, for instance, *Kipling and "Orientalism*," B. J. Moore-Gilbert's examination of
British literary representations of India in the second half of the nineteenth century,
a study that presents an admirably self-conscious critique of, and at least partial corrective to, Said's totalizing impulse.

15. On American involvement in the Chinese opium trade, see Walker, *Opium and
Foreign Policy*, chap. 1; and for an overview of the sentiment against that involvement
at home, see Morgan, *Drugs in America*, 7. On the history of opium smoking in
America, see Courtwright, *Dark Paradise*, chap. 3; and for an assessment of American
reactions to Chinese smokers, see Musto, *The American Disease*, 3–6.

16. See, for instance, the bereaved husband of Ligeia, who revels "in the excitement of
my opium dreams (for I was habitually fettered in the shackles of the drug)" while
he pictures his lost love whose eyes were "even fuller than the fullest of the gazelle
eyes of the tribe of the valley of Nourjahad." The narrator of "The Fall of the House
of Usher" similarly alludes to the De Quinceyan "after-dream of the reveller upon
opium—the bitter lapse into every-day life—the hideous dropping off of the veil,"
and he compares Roderick Usher's languid manner to that of "the irreclaimable
eater of opium." Poe himself has often been mythologized as a romantically excessive opium eater, largely because of the influence of the sensationalized biography
published days after his death by his literary executor, Rufus Griswold.

17. Morgan, *Drugs in America*, 54. Morgan also notes the two authors' towering influence on American writing about opium. For representative examples of such writings, see William Blair's "An Opium Eater in America" (1842) and Fitz Hugh Ludlow's *The Hasheesh Eater* (1857). See Morgan, *Drugs in America*, 184 n.45, for a more
extensive list of such derivative writings.

18. Courtwright, *Dark Paradise*, x. Although Courtwright questions whether De
Quincey's accounts of opium use influenced the actual habits of the average American opium user, he nonetheless affirms that the English author was a pervasive presence in American writing about opium (ibid., 59) and, as I have mentioned, notes
that he had a significant influence on perceptions of opium use if not on the details
of that use itself.

19. Mezzrow and Wolfe, *Really the Blues*, 97. The association persists elsewhere in the

genre of jazz autobiography as well. Art Pepper, who was imprisoned several times for heroin possession, recounts his time "in jail with a chinaman," with whom the paradigmatic process of infection is interestingly reversed: "He had been shooting 'black' [opium] for years and years. Chinese didn't get busted for a long time because the Chinese as a whole are much stronger than the whites and the blacks. But then some of the Chinese got out and started shooting regular heroin, hanging out with the other dope fiends, and they got Americanized" (Pepper, *Straight Life*, 139, brackets sic).

20. Burroughs, *Junky*, 5, 12, 6, 58, 111–12. The same kinds of associations surround cannabis, which Baudelaire claimed "comes to us from the Orient; the stimulating properties of hemp were well known in ancient Egypt, and its use under different names is widespread in India, Algeria, and Arabia" (Baudelaire, "from 'The Poem of Hashish,'" 36). In the tradition of representations of East End opium dens, H. H. Kane's early twentieth-century hashish-house in New York is a "scene of Oriental magnificence" (Kane, "A Hashish-House," 165), and is echoed in the Avalon Ballroom of 1960s San Francisco described by rock musician John Densmore: "With most of the packed-in audience lazing on the floor rather than dancing—it looked like a dope den with the marijuana smoke swirling in the air" while the "people seemed entranced by the Oriental tuning" of the Doors's psychedelic rock anthem "The End" (Densmore, *Riders on the Storm*, 108–9).

21. For an account of the origins of LSD, its connections to other drugs, and its complex cultural legacy, see Stevens, *Storming Heaven*.

22. Hofmann, "from *LSD: My Problem Child*," 80.

23. Nin, "from *The Diary*," 143.

24. Witkiewicz, "Report about the Effects of Peyote," 234–35. Aldous Huxley similarly imports Oriental associations into his mescaline experience, speaking in such images as "the Dharma Body," and so on, (Huxley, "The Doors of Perception," 45).

25. George Bush listed the goals of the invasion as "to safeguard the lives of Americans, to defend democracy in Panama, to combat drug trafficking and to protect the integrity of the Panama Canal treaty," setting the tone for even less mediated linkages, such as Les Aspin's statement that "the test . . . of the question is, have we disrupted the drug trade . . . and have we established democracy?" (Towell and Felton, "Invasion," 3534–35.).

26. See, for instance, "Every Agent's a Drug Agent" and Davidson, "Can Soldiers Stop Drugs?"

27. Musto, "Opium, Cocaine, and Marijuana," 40.

28. Sedgwick, *Between Men*, 18.

29. See, for instance, Gagnier, *Subjectivities*.

30. Eliot, *Middlemarch*, 109.

31. Lowborough himself runs the gamut of obvious addictions: apart from excessive gambling and laudanum use, "he soon discovered that the demon of drink was nearly as black as the demon of play, and nearly as hard to get rid of" (Brontë, *The Tenant of Wildfell Hall*, 203). Much of the fourth chapter of *The Tenant of Wildfell Hall* is given over to a debate over whether alcohol is a blessing or a curse, and whether its intemperate use is the result of nature or nurture.

32. Brantlinger, *Rule of Darkness*, 12–13. This thesis is elaborated in Daniel Bivona, *Desire and Contradiction*.

33. See, for instance, John Drew's chapter, "Coleridge: 'Kubla Khan,' and the Rise of Tantric Buddhism." John Livingston Lowes's famous *The Road to Xanadu* also chronicles Coleridge's extensive Orientalist reading.

34. For a more detailed discussion of Coleridge's sense of the East as the wellspring of all religions and his plans to write an Orientalist epic, see Shaffer, *"Kubla Khan" and the Fall of Jerusalem.*

35. De Quincey, *Confessions,* 108–9.

36. "East London Opium Smokers," 68–72.

Chapter 1

1. Baumgart, *Imperialism,* 3.

2. Brantlinger, *Rule of Darkness,* 21, 7.

3. Philips, *The East India Company,* 32.

4. Daniel Bivona argues that Disraeli's expansionist ideology is already evident in his trilogy of novels written during the hungry forties, a work that "promotes the expansion of England as the inevitable extension of the project of finding a place for the middle and working classes in the governing structure of the country." But, says Bivona, "Disraeli felt he could only sell the idea of geographical expansion to the 'Little Englanders' if he could justify imperialism as an attempt to restore an ancient unity in the modern era"—that is, the original unity of all Western civilizations with their origins in the Orient (Bivona, *Desire and Contradiction,* 3). Disraeli thus casts in a positive light what De Quincey sees as the corrosive force undermining British identity: the supposed Oriental origins of Western civilization.

5. Seeley, *The Expansion of England,* 12.

6. Reynolds, *Modes of Imperialism,* 1.

7. As John Tomlinson points out, there is hardly any commonly used phrase more slippery to define than "cultural imperialism," composed as it is of two terms that are themselves evasive. But he helpfully notes that, in general, "in the case of the concept of cultural imperialism, culture is used in distinction from the *political* and *economic* spheres of life which are the concern of 'imperialism' in its more general sense" (Tomlinson, *Cultural Imperialism,* 5).

8. See, for instance, Catherine Hall's discussion of the construction of various versions of "Englishness" around Baptist missionary activities in Jamaica in the 1830s and '40s (Hall, "Missionary Stories") and Gauri Viswanathan's account of the role of the institutionalized study of English literature in Britain's rule of India *(Masks of Conquest).*

9. Reynolds, *Modes of Imperialism,* 1.

10. See Green, *Dreams of Adventure;* and Cheyfitz, *The Poetics of Imperialism.*

11. Bivona, *Desire and Contradiction,* viii.

12. I deliberately pepper this assertion with qualifiers, for "the Orient" is a shifting, unstable concept in the nineteenth century, though it is not always treated as such, as I will discuss in more depth below.

13. Said, *Orientalism,* 50.

14. It was from such Oriental tales and travel narratives that writers such as Coleridge, De Quincey, Dickens, and countless others drew their formative impressions and provisional definitions of the Orient, and they in turn mediated and modified them

for new audiences. Coleridge, for instance, spoke of the significant and lasting influence of the Oriental tales he read as a child: "from my early reading of Faery Tales and Genii &c &c—my mind had been habituated *to the Vast*—& I never regarded *my senses* in any way as the criteria of my belief" (Coleridge, *Collected Letters*, 1:354). Likewise, De Quincey claimed that the *Arabian Nights* "fixed and fascinated my gaze, in a degree that I never afterwards forgot, and did not at that time comprehend" (De Quincey, "Autobiography," 128). Dickens also attests to the grip the *Arabian Nights* had on the average English schoolboy's imagination with Scrooge's fond remembrance of Ali Baba and other characters from Scheherezade's narratives as tangible friends of his childhood.

15. For much of this information, I am indebted to two essays: Hugh Honour's "The Vision of Cathay" and Arthur O. Lovejoy's "The Chinese Origin of a Romanticism."

16. Collis, *Foreign Mud*, 16.

17. Kabbani, *Europe's Myth of Orient*, 11.

18. These figures are from Berridge and Edwards, *Opium and the People*, table 1, 272–73. I am indebted to Berridge and Edwards for much of the factual information in this chapter about opium use in nineteenth-century England.

19. Quoted in Berridge and Edwards, *Opium and the People*, 174.

20. Apart from Quakers, Anglican and nonconformist clergy represented the largest share of the SSOT's membership, and the parliamentarian Lord Shaftesbury was its president from 1881 to 1895.

21. Kendal Black Drop was one of many brands of opium preparations Coleridge used during his long addiction. Another was Braithwaite's Lancashire Genuine Black Drop. Latimer and Goldberg interestingly note that Braithwaite's made their preparation from " 'the best Turkey opium dried,' and steeped it for days in saffron, cloves, and powerful *acetic acid*. The resulting nonalcoholic suspension was advertised as four times the strength of ordinary laudanum, and that was probably a modest claim. . . . prolonged acetylation of the morphine content of Lancashire Genuine Black Drop must have converted a good fraction of it into straight heroin" (Latimer and Goldberg, *Flowers in the Blood*, 79).

22. Berridge and Edwards, *Opium and the People*, 32–34, 66–72.

23. Charles Newman, *The Evolution of Medical Education*, 2–3.

24. Of the many opiates (alkaloids of opium), morphine is the most powerful—opium's "active ingredient" one might say. First isolated in 1803, morphine was in wide medical use by the 1840s and was administered by the new technology of hypodermic injection beginning in the 1860s. Perhaps the most familiar opiate besides morphine is codeine, known today for its common use as a prescription cough suppressant and pain reliever. All opiates are associated to some degree with tolerance and withdrawal.

25. Dr. Clifford Allbutt, quoted in Berridge and Edwards, *Opium and the People*, 142.

26. The main forum for debate and development of British disease theories of addiction was the *British Journal of Inebriety*, the organ of Dr. Norman Kerr's Society for the Study of Inebriety, which in its earliest manifestation as the Society for Promoting Legislation for the Control and Cure of Habitual Drunkards (1876) was instrumental in passing the 1878 Habitual Drunkards Act (Berridge and Edwards, *Opium and the People*, 151–52.). Both alcoholism and morphinism had significant moral compo-

nents and were thus exceptions to existing models of supposedly physiological diseases such as typhoid and cholera. The two exceptions were usually grouped together as special "diseases of the will" and subsumed under the rubric of "inebriety" or "addiction."

27. Berridge and Edwards, *Opium and the People*, 158.
28. Dr. S. A. K. Strahan, quoted in Berridge and Edwards, *Opium and the People*, 145.
29. Hayter, *Opium and the Romantic Imagination*, 38.
30. Berridge and Edwards, *Opium and the People*, 50.
31. De Quincey, *Confessions*, 78.
32. Ibid., 31.
33. Ibid., 31–32.
34. Quoted in Berridge and Edwards, *Opium and the People*, 105–6.
35. It has long been speculated that Keats was dependent upon laudanum during his final illness with tuberculosis, and recent evidence has supported the hypothesis. A team of researchers under the supervision of Ronald K. Siegel analyzed strands from a lock of Keats's hair saved by Leigh Hunt and preserved at the University of Iowa: "Using a sensitive chemical procedure known as radioimmunoassay," says Siegel, "we found morphine in massive amounts. Keats was not only a user, he was probably dependent on the drug as well" (Siegel, *Intoxication*, 127).
36. Berridge and Edwards, *Opium and the People*, 201–2.
37. Quoted in Berridge and Edwards, *Opium and the People*, 198.
38. See, for instance, Colley, "Whose Nation?"; Cottrell, "The Devil on Two Sticks"; Ross, "Romancing the Nation-State"; Brennan, "The National Longing"; Hobsbawm, *Nations and Nationalism;* and Benedict Anderson, *Imagined Communities.*
39. As Timothy Brennan says, "The rise of the modern nation-state in Europe in the late eighteenth and early nineteenth centuries is inseparable from the forms and subjects of imaginative literature. On the one hand, the political tasks of modern nationalism directed the course of literature, leading through the Romantic concepts of 'folk character' and 'national language' to the (largely illusory) divisions of literature into distinct 'national literatures'. On the other hand, and just as fundamentally, literature participated in the formation of nations through the creation of 'national print media'—the newspaper and the novel" (Brennan, "The National Longing," 48). Brennan thus echoes and elaborates on Benedict Anderson, who says, "the novel and the newspaper . . . provided the technical means for 're-presenting' the *kind* of imagined community that is the nation" (Benedict Anderson, *Imagined Communities,* 25). See also Colley, "Whose Nation?" 100–3.
40. Cottrell, "The Devil on Two Sticks," 263.
41. Ibid., 265.
42. Hobsbawm, *Nations and Nationalism,* 38.
43. Ross, "Romancing the Nation-State," 56–57.
44. Ibid., 57.
45. Ibid., 70.

Chapter 2

1. Coleridge, "Lectures," 226.
2. Ibid., 225–26.

3. Idem., *Collected Letters,* 2: 1006.

4. Unless otherwise noted, all references to Coleridge's poems in this chapter are to the versions printed in Ernest Hartley Coleridge's edition of the *Complete Poetical Works.* Passages from poems are cited by line number, and quotes from the verse drama *Osorio* are cited by page number.

5. Mary Astell, *A Serious Proposal to the Ladies* (London, 1694), quoted in Perry, "Colonizing the Breast," 221–22. Perry also quotes from the *Spectator* of December 12, 1711, in which Richard Steele questions whether the wet-nursed infant might not "imbibe the gross Humours and Qualities of the Nurse, like a Plant in a different Ground, or like a Graft upon a different Stalk?" He resorts to what became a common analogy: "Do we not observe, that a Lamb sucking a Goat changes very much its Nature, nay even its Skin and Wooll into the Goat kind?" (ibid., 221).

6. The emphasis changed after the influential William Cadogan exhorted fathers in 1748 to insist that mothers nurse their own children so that their whole upbringing could be superintended directly. Rousseau's *Émile* (1762) helped give currency to the sentiment that, whether the child was nursed at home or out of doors, every child should remain under the care of the same guardian throughout childhood. See Fildes, *Wet Nursing,* chap. 8. For the revival of contamination fears in the nineteenth century, see Nead, *Myths of Sexuality,* 27; and Roberts, "Mothers and Babies."

7. Flora Ann Steel and G. Gardiner, *The Complete Indian Housekeeper and Cook* (1888), quoted in Chaudhouri, "Memsahibs and Motherhood," 529.

8. Coleridge, *Collected Letters,* 1: 354.

9. Ibid., 1: 348.

10. Ibid., 1: 347.

11. Ibid., 1: 350.

12. Although I would be suspicious of a uniform approach that would see all dales as vaginas and all mountains as breasts, Coleridge's characterization of the isle as mother and his more insistent sexualization of the Oriental landscape in "Kubla Khan" make such readings all but obvious. Indeed there is already a long tradition of psychoanalytic readings of Coleridge's landscapes as female bodies, beginning as early as 1934 with Maud Bodkin's assertion that her own response to "Kubla Khan" "is a brooding wonder at the water's movement, and sympathy with it as with a thing alive." She says that "The same reflections apply to the consideration of the cavern image," in which she looks for a "trace of reference to the womb" (Bodkin, *Archetypal Patterns in Poetry,* 108–10).

13. The 1816 preface cites the substance only as "an anodyne," but the Crewe Manuscript of the poem is more explicit, referring to "two grains of opium." Coleridge took his opium usually in the form of laudanum (Coleridge, "Crew MS of 'Kubla Khan.'").

14. Purchas, *Purchas his Pilgrimage,* 415. The chapter in which this passage appears, "Of the Religions of the Tartars, and Cathayans" (bk. 4, chap. 13), tells of worship practices centered primarily on deities associated with milk, such as one represented by "a thing of Felt fashioned like a Dugge" (ibid., 411), and on the household idols representing the Tartars themselves: "Next to the doore on the womens side . . . there is an Image with a Cowes Udder for the women, whose office it is to milke the Kine; on the other side another with a Mares Udder for the men" (ibid., 413–14).

15. Obligated under ancient Hebrew patriarchal law to produce heirs through sexual

intercourse with his brother's widow, Onan nonetheless refuses: "Onan knew that the seed should not be his; and it came to pass, when he went in unto his brother's wife, that he spilled it on the ground" (Genesis 38: 9–10). The irate Yahweh strikes him dead for his defiance. The fact that Kubla "spendeth" as well as "poureth" the liquid further reinforces its resemblance to semen, for orgasm is of course a common connotation of "spend" in Purchas's seventeenth-century English. In Purchas's account of the Tartar religion, the pouring forth of any liquids upon the ground is associated with severe penalties when practiced by a commoner: "they reckon these things following to be sinnes . . . to powre out meat, milke, or any kinde of drinke upon the ground; or to make water within the Tabernacle, which whosoever doeth willingly is slaine" (Purchas, *Purchas his Pilgrimage,* 412).

16. M. H. Abrams even titled his monograph on putatively opium-inspired imagery in eighteenth- and early nineteenth-century poetry *The Milk of Paradise.*

17. As mentioned in chapter 1, the bulk of opium consumed in nineteenth-century England came from Turkey, but the drug was nonetheless broadly associated with a more comprehensive and undifferentiated "Orient" in the culture of the period.

18. Kubla Khan had already been mythologized by Marco Polo as the supreme imperialist long before Coleridge took him on: "in respect to number of subjects, extent of territory, and amount of revenue," said Polo, "he surpasses every sovereign that has heretofore been or that now is in the world." Polo was also awed by the Khan's successful unification within this empire of diverse religions, an accomplishment that would have impressed Coleridge as well, with his interest in a time- and space-transcendent religious and cultural unity in the East. Polo even answers to the fondest wishes of Coleridge, the German Higher Critics, and the Unitarians as he concludes that, despite his lip service to Islam, Judaism, and "the idolaters" as well as Christianity, "from the manner in which his majesty acted towards them, it is evident that he regarded the faith of the Christians as the truest and the best" (quoted in Benedict Anderson, *Imagined Communities,* 16–17).

19. J. B. Beer also reads this passage as a quasi-sexual union, but at a level abstract enough to obscure the ambiguous gender roles of the fluids and earthly orifices. He says that "the river and the cavern are themselves male and female symbols," and that their deployment in "Kubla Khan" is consistent with an archetypal pattern in which "after the Fall, the male principle, separated from the female, seeks eternally to unite with her again, in order that they may mingle in the creative fountain, and recover the lost glory" (Beer, *Coleridge the Visionary,* 210–12).

20. Coleridge, *Collected Letters,* 1: 209.

21. The ad hoc nature of Coleridge's Brahman Creed is especially evident here: its principal image of Vishnu sitting on the lotus flower is Hindu, but its chief spokesperson is the Moslem Alhadra. The confusion illustrates the degree to which any subgroups of "the Orient" were problematically differentiated for Coleridge.

22. Coleridge, *Collected Letters,* 1: 250.

23. Coleridge, *Notebooks,* entry 848.

24. Plato, *Ion,* quoted in Schneider, *Coleridge, Opium and Kubla Khan,* 245–46.

25. Said speaks of *The Bacchae* as one of the first available specimens of European Orientalism, manifesting a proto-Coleridgean anxiety about "the motif of the Orient as insinuating danger": "Rationality is undermined by Eastern excesses, those mysteriously attractive opposites to what seem to be normal values. The difference between

East and West is symbolized by the sternness with which, at first, Pentheus rejects the hysterical bacchantes. When later he himself becomes a bacchant, he is destroyed not so much for having given in to Dionysus [whom Said brands as Oriental] as for having incorrectly assessed Dionysus's menace in the first place. The lesson that Euripides intends is . . . [that] there is such a thing as judgment . . . which means sizing up correctly the force of alien powers and correctly coming to terms with them" (Said, *Orientalism*, 57). In this light, Coleridge is not so much like the bacchic maidens as he is like the presumptuous Pentheus, who dabbles with Oriental mysteries only to be possessed and destroyed by them.

26. See, for instance, Spivak, who says that "both as object of colonialist historiography and as subject of insurgency, the ideological construction of gender keeps the male dominant. If, in the context of colonial production, the subaltern has no history and cannot speak, the subaltern as female is even more deeply in shadow" (Spivak, "Can the Subaltern Speak?" 287). Others argue that the imperial order was inherently repressive of *British* women as well. "Living on an elite island that was nevertheless rife with domestic politics, dwelling in a protection hysterically conscious of how much protection was necessary," says Suleri, "the Anglo-Indian woman persistently became a symbolic casualty to the deranging costs of colonial power" (Suleri, *The Rhetoric of English India*, 74).

27. Miller, *The Novel and the Police*, 152, 166, 181. Miller speaks specifically of Wilkie Collins's *The Woman in White*, in which he says the male containment of the female awakens homosexual panic partly because it is reminiscent of the late-century formulation of male homosexuality as "a woman's soul trapped in a man's body" (ibid., 154–55). But such a sense of gay identity as a matter of being invisibly of the opposite gender, though possibly playing around the edges of Coleridge's late-eighteenth-century sense of ambiguous gender roles, was not yet readily available in such a clearly codified formulation when Coleridge wrote. As Louis Crompton details, late eighteenth- and early nineteenth-century representations of homosexuality were at least thickly veiled and, as in the case of Byron, were often associated with a classical Hellenic ideal of male-male relationships. Yet, as also in the case of Byron, male homosexuality was associated with the Orient as well, a cultural possibility that may also have been available to Coleridge (Crompton, *Byron and Greek Love*).

28. There was already ample precedent for seeing the British colonial relationship with the Orient, especially India, in terms of rape. Edmund Burke famously couched his indictment of Warren Hastings, for instance, in terms of both metaphorical and actual rape (see Paxton, *Mobilizing Chivalry*, 5–6).

Chapter 3

1. Lindop, "Lamb, Hazlitt, and De Quincey," 129.
2. Unless otherwise noted, all references to the *Confessions* are by page number to Hayter's edition of the 1821 version.

Other critics have similarly explored ways in which De Quincey is implicitly deconstructive. See, for instance, Sedgwick's exploration of the recurrent unstable "within/without" pairing ("Language as Live Burial"), and Bruss on the ways in which, throughout De Quincey's writings, "what had seemed to be the center was actually the periphery" (Bruss, *Autobiographical Acts*, 109).

3. In fact, as Grevel Lindop also notes, a significant manifestation of De Quincey's general torment is his anxiety about how to define himself in opposition specifically to *Coleridge:* "at times De Quincey seems to perceive Coleridge as a kind of double. He is preoccupied above all by the fact that Coleridge is another literary opium-addict, and can thus function either as an extenuating parallel or as a threat . . . 'The greatest man that has ever appeared' has become merely a case of 'oneself repeated once too often'" (Lindop, "Lamb, Hazlitt, and De Quincey," 131). For a more in-depth consideration of De Quincey's conflicted sense of identification with and need for differentiation from the older poet, see Leask, "Murdering One's Double."

4. Unless otherwise noted, references to De Quincey's works other than the 1821 *Confessions* are to Masson's edition of the *Collected Writings* and are cited parenthetically in the text as *CW,* volume:page number. Titles of essays thus cited are included in the Works Cited.

5. Barrell, *The Infection,* 16. De Quincey's vexed relationship with opium is a prime example of this pattern: "the phrase 'English Opium-Eater' itself can be read as an example of inoculation . . . to describe oneself as an 'eater' of opium was to claim kinship with a recognisable Turkish identity—a kinship qualified, however, and made safe, by the adjective 'English'" (ibid., 17).

6. Ibid., 16–17.

7. Barrell argues that "the opening section of 'The English Mail-Coach' . . . seems to function as the architectural plan for a system of fortification which is normally to be found only as an archaeological ruin, as the trace of an overwhelming defeat at the hands of a persistent and ferocious invader" (ibid., 17). He thus implies that the invasion/infection was a fait accompli long before the beginning of De Quincey's battle against it, but he nonetheless still assumes a prelapsarian division with the scenario of an "invader" destroying a "fortification."

8. *The Patriot Briton—or England's Invasion,* quoted in Cottrell, "The Devil on Two Sticks," 263. This "idealisation of continuity," says Cottrell, "was the fulcrum upon which the very notion of British identity turned" (ibid., 263). The British construction of national identity is thus a specific manifestation of the more general phenomenon noted by Benedict Anderson: "If nation-states are widely conceded to be 'new' and 'historical,' the notions to which they give political expression always loom out of an immemorial past, and, still more important, glide into a limitless future" (Benedict Anderson, *Imagined Communities,* 11–12).

9. According to roughly contemporary merchants' usage cited in the *Oxford English Dictionary.*

10. This ideal of steadfast stability was a commonplace of nineteenth-century Orientalism. Said avers that "the Orient was overvalued for its pantheism, its spirituality, *its stability, its longevity,* its primitivity and so forth" (Said, *Orientalism,* 150, emphasis mine).

11. See, for instance, Cottrell, "The Devil on Two Sticks."

12. Bivona, *Desire and Contradiction,* 3. The idea of the British Empire as a means of reinforcing class hierarchies is a common one and is often imagined in terms of buttressing the aristocracy as well as the middle classes. Bivona argues that "Empire, in Disraeli's view, fashions gentlemen of substance out of erstwhile bored aristocrats, thus providing a small measure of justification for the social and political privileges of a class which expends wealth but does not, in nineteenth-century eyes, seem to

produce much of it" (ibid., 110). Benedict Anderson similarly finds it tempting "to argue that the existence of late colonial empires even served to *shore up* domestic aristocratic bastions, since they appeared to confirm on a global, modern stage, antique conceptions of power and privilege" (Benedict Anderson, *Imagined Communities,* 150). Hannah Arendt, however, sees imperialism primarily as an inevitable extension of markets, resources, and domains for the mercantile classes: "Imperialism was born when the ruling class in capitalist production came up against national limitations to its economic necessity; for if it did not want to give up the capitalist system whose inherent law is constant economic growth, it had to impose this law upon its home governments and to proclaim expansion to be an ultimate political goal of foreign policy" (Arendt, *The Origins of Totalitarianism,* 126).

13. Although the Indian venture is perhaps the most obvious antecedent, there were certainly other earlier colonial trading projects in which many of these students' fathers were involved as well. While De Quincey's uncle was a colonel in the Military Service of the East India Company in Bengal, for instance, his father the linen merchant got his wares primarily from the colonies of Ireland and the West Indies (Lindop, *The Opium-Eater,* 1, 123).

14. De Quincey, "Canton Expedition," 687.

15. Ibid.

16. Even the Orientalness of the crocodile-coachman is at least equivocal, however: his wearing the livery of the English mail-coach once again establishes a tension of identity between inside (the crocodile's body) and outside (the uniform he wears).

17. In the scenario I outline here, De Quincey's opium experience exposes that most Britons had it wrong with their conception of British imperialism in the East as a process of progressively dominating the Orient. Nigel Leask has offered a similar insight, arguing that opium is associated for De Quincey with "a nightmare realization that [England] has become economically dependent on (or addicted to) its subjugated Other"(Leask, *British Romantic Writers,* 9). What I ultimately want to emphasize, though, is De Quincey's cataclysmic realization of the non-differentiation of East and West that ultimately renders any such hierarchy meaningless.

18. "During the summer of 1803, De Quincey had spent much time debating with his Uncle Thomas the rights and wrongs of British rule in India. Thomas Penson was ready to bow to Mrs. Quincey's view that the British had no moral right to be there; young Thomas De Quincey, on the other hand, defended their presence" (Lindop, *The Opium-Eater,* 123). He was also later to defend the opium wars in print and to urge ever more aggressive military measures all the way to the colonization of China.

19. Lady Carbery, who, as De Quincey says in the *Confessions,* gave him the ten guineas that enabled him to run away from Manchester Grammar School, was heir to Colonel Henry Watson, who made his fortune as "one of the original entrepreneurs who urged on the Company the daring policy of smuggling Bengal opium into China" (Lindop, *The Opium-Eater,* 123–24).

20. The imagery is, perhaps not coincidentally, reminiscent of the latter portion of "Kubla Khan" and shares its implicit sexual aspects.

21. De Quincey was writing in the middle of an era burgeoning with geological theories about the derivation of the world, theories that caused widespread crises in conceptions of time, history, and origins. As Richard Altick says, "the evidence of geology

and paleontology had been mounting since the middle of the eighteenth century. 'The testimony of the rocks,' to use the title of a popular early Victorian book, challenged the simple Biblical formulation of terrestrial history. The older geological interpretation, that of the so-called catastrophic school, was that the fossils of extinct species found embedded in rock strata were evidence of cataclysms—floods, earthquakes, devastating volcanic eruptions. . . . A newer theory, set forth in Sir Charles Lyell's *Principles of Geology* (1830–33), was the uniformitarian. Discarding the premise of catastrophes, it maintained that the causes of geological change in the remote past were no different than those still operative in the nineteenth century—the slow, ceaseless action of wind and water, the elevation and depression of land masses. Such an assumption, of course, also required extending the chronology into veritable eons, . . . and the miniature scale of history explicit in the Old Testament was accordingly rendered all the more incredible" (Altick, *Victorian People and Ideas,* 222–23).

22. An ayah was a female Indian servant to British masters, often a lady's maid or nurse-maid (see Visram, *Ayahs, Lascars, and Princes,* chap. 2). De Quincey's nursery scenario also recalls the colonial fear of Indian nurses and contamination of English children through their milk discussed in chapter 2.

23. See chapter 1 for a discussion of these phenomena.

24. Freud, "Beyond the Pleasure Principle," 14.

25. Ibid., 7–8.

26. An intuitive expansion of this model would then suggest that De Quincey's writing is an adjunct of his addiction, yet another means besides opium by which he can repeatedly relive the excitement (whether positive or negative) of nondifferentiation even as he tries to counteract it.

27. The transition from De Quincey's writings to a discussion in the next chapter of Wilkie Collins's *The Moonstone* (1868) may seem silently to leap over a gap of several decades, as De Quincey published his most enduringly famous work, the *Confessions,* in 1821 and is commonly categorized as a late Romantic. But in fact De Quincey was writing until the day of his death in 1859, arguably placing him more in the Victorian than the Romantic era. His later works include meditations on the 1857 Indian Mutiny that continued to develop the trajectories traced in this chapter, and "The English Mail-Coach," which originally appeared in 1849 but was subject to De Quincey's repeated tinkering through 1854. These mature works as well as the *Confessions* significantly influenced later writers and thinkers about opium. Otherwise, the gap is a very real one: most of the writings about opium and the Orient published between the 1820s and the 1860s treat only debates about the controversial Indo-Chinese trade and deal little or not at all with the actual use of opium in England.

Chapter 4

1. All references to *The Moonstone* are cited parenthetically in the text by page number of J. I. M. Stewart's edition.

2. Although there has generally been a critical resistance—or at best indifference—to seeing *The Moonstone* as historically referential, it has nonetheless been noted before that the Moonstone irresistibly parallels India in many significant respects. John R.

Reed points out that the main action of the novel takes place in 1848–49, "the time of the second Anglo-Sikh War in India, which established British control over that country with great certainty through annexation of the vast areas of the Punjab" (Reed, "English Imperialism," 286), and that Collins acknowledged in his preface to the first edition that a model for the Moonstone was the famous Koh-i-Noor diamond, which "came into the possession of the English royal family as a portion of the Indian settlement after the Anglo-Sikh War of 1848–49 [when it was] presented to Queen Victoria at a great reception in St. James's Palace in 1850 to mark the two hundred and fiftieth anniversary of the founding of the East India Company" (ibid., 287). In Reed's reading of *The Moonstone*, "individual greed . . . is emblematic of a far greater crime;" "it is a national not a personal guilt that is in question in this novel, and national rather than individual values that are tested" (ibid., 284, 288).

3. Wheeler, *India of the Vedic Age*, v.

4. Quoted in Wilbur, *The East India Company*, 360.

5. Tipu himself was also the subject of a strange and ambivalent British fascination. As Barrell says, "from the early 1790's and for more than thirty years after his death in 1799, a curious cult status was accorded to Tipu in Britain, and he became 'firmly embedded in . . . nursery folklore' as the oriental tiger the British loved to hate" (Barrell, *The Infection of Thomas De Quincey*, 50). Tipu's cult status was due in part to the huge popularity of a strange objet d'art brought back to England from Seringapatam after his defeat, a moving sculpture complete with sound effects known popularly as "Tippoo's Tiger." In keeping with the cultural currents described in this chapter, British fascination with this strange object smacks almost of a collective national masochism, as it represents Tipu's emblematic mascot, an Indian tiger, devouring a British subject. Tipu also appeared again and again throughout the first half of the century as the villain in plays and fiction including the novel *Tippoo Sultaun* (1840), the second commercial success of Captain Philip Meadows Taylor, author of the popular *Confessions of a Thug* (1839).

6. The quote is from an account printed in Collins's chief source for the history of the siege, Theodore Hook's *The Life of General, the Right Honourable Sir David Baird*, 197.

7. Wilbur, *The East India Company*, 360. See also Reed's situation of the Moonstone vis-á-vis the presentation of the Koh-i-Noor diamond to Queen Victoria after English victory in the Second Anglo-Sikh War (n. 2 above).

8. The phrase was first made popular by a speech Robert Clive delivered in the House of Commons on May 10, 1773: "let me conclude by observing that Bengal is the brightest jewel in the British Crown, though at present in a rude and unpolished state, that if it be once properly improved and burnished it will eclipse everything of the kind that has yet been seen in the world but if it be once suffered to drop out and be lost, the crown will lose half its splendor and dignity" (*Parliamentary Debates* 6, quoted in Yapp, "The Brightest Jewel," 35). But even earlier (1772), one William Bolts, arguing for replacement of the Company by the Crown, had spoken of "Hindoostan, which, with proper management, might be rendered the richest jewel in the British Crown, by being made an inexhaustable source of extensive commerce, maritime power and national wealth" (*Considerations on Indian Affairs*, quoted in Yapp, "The Brightest Jewel," 37).

9. When the British East India Company ceased to be a commercial body in 1833, it officially became instead what it had been tending toward since the middle of the

previous century, a governing body complete with its own civil service and an army composed of British officers commanding Indian soldiers known as sepoys. This organization ruled approximately two-thirds of India until a number of sepoys mutinied against their British commanders in 1857. The mutiny was finally "put down," but the East India Company was subsequently dissolved, and India was placed under direct British rule through an official secretary of state. Collins's critiques of the Mutiny are embodied in two pieces for Dickens's *All The Year Round*, "A Sermon for Sepoys," in which he castigates "the human tigers" of India as "Betrayers and Assassins," and the obvious fictional restaging of the mutiny in the West Indies he co-authored with Dickens called "The Perils of Certain English Prisoners."

10. Brantlinger, *Rule of Darkness*, 204. These particular terms arise from one incident that took place during the Mutiny and received extensive attention in England, the "massacre" at Cawnpore, in which Nana Sahib ordered the execution of hundreds of English women and children after leading them to believe they would be released. Brantlinger argues that all popular accounts of the Mutiny in general concentrated on Cawnpore in particular: "Nana Sahib's treachery serves as a reductive synecdoche for the entire rebellion—one that is its own instant explanation, transforming politics into crime and widespread social forces into questions of race and personality" (203). Such accounts—including poems, novels, plays, and histories—numbered in the hundreds between 1857 and World War II, with the greatest concentration in the fifteen or so years after the Mutiny.

11. Nancy L. Paxton argues that the insistence in popular Mutiny narratives on the rape of Englishwomen by Indian men—which firsthand accounts suggest occurred at nothing approaching the rate upon which popular narratives insist—marks an important third stage in a shift from (1) Edmund Burke's minority outcry against both the metaphorical rape of India and the actual rape of Indian women by English colonialists to (2) a concentration in popular Oriental tales on the rape of Indian women by Indian men to (3) with the Mutiny narratives, the rape of Englishwomen by Indian men. This shift, she argues, in part does the ideological work of attempting to control "anxiety about increasing racial conflict in India" and "a profound crisis in definitions of gender roles and sexual identity at home" (Paxton, "Mobilizing Chivalry," 20).

12. Sue Lonoff notes that "when Franklin Blake steals into Rachel's room at night and surreptitiously removes the Moonstone from her cabinet, she loses her most precious possession. Eventually she compensates by marrying him and becoming pregnant, but her jewel is irrevocably lost to her. Recalling the Victorian maxim that a young girl's virginity is her most precious possession, and the statement in the prologue that the diamond waxes and wanes on a lunar cycle . . . the theft is a symbolic defloration" (Lonoff, *Wilkie Collins*, 210). (See also Charles Rycroft's psychoanalytical reading of the novel, *Imagination and Reality*, 119–22.) If one extends this logic into the scenario of the hidden Indian stealing the gem, the equation with the supposed rapes deplored in tirades against the Indian Mutiny is all but obvious.

13. Such critics found their most frequent and representative expression in the organ of the Society for the Suppression of the Opium Trade, *The Friend of China*, articles from which will figure importantly in the discussions to come in chapters 5 and 6.

14. An understated current eddying around Rachel ties her more directly to the Orient. The three Brahmins make their first appearance in the novel with an implicit echo

of De Quincey's Malay visitor. De Quincey's scene is one of vivid contrasts: "In a cottage kitchen . . . panelled on the wall with dark wood . . . stood the Malay—his turban and loose trousers of dingy white relieved upon the dark panelling," and his skin "enamelled or veneered with mahogany" (De Quincey, *Confessions*, 90–91). Collins's Orientals similarly make their first appearance as "three mahogany-coloured Indians, in white frocks and trousers" (ibid., 48). Rachel also appears in scenes of such heightened visual contrast, as when Betteredge first sees her after the disappearance of the Moonstone: "There, on the threshold of her bedroom door, stood Miss Rachel, almost as white in the face as the white dressing-gown that clothed her. There also stood the two doors of the India cabinet, wide open" (ibid., 115). While her extreme whiteness places her in stark contrast to the dark wooden India cabinet in the background, the terms of the contrast echo those that were contained within the "three mahogany-coloured Indians, in white frocks and trousers," and thus arguably implicate her *within* rather than *against* a representation of India.

Chapter 5

1. For an historical overview of the anti-opium movement, see chapter 1.
2. Piercy, "Opium Smoking in London," 239–40.
3. The rhetoric linking opium and perdition is evident even in the earliest published accounts of opium dens. One of these presents opium smoking as a parallel phenomenon to gin and laudanum drinking, "moral scourges" that already are "hurrying myriads into perdition" ("In an Opium Den," 198). The anonymous author interestingly also sees laudanum drinking as a contagious plague spread by insidious immigrants, but in this case immigrants from the Midlands to London.
4. See, for instance, de Mas, "Translation"; Alcock, "Sir Rutherford Alcock's Paper"; and Turner, "Letters."
5. Choo, *The Chinese in London*, 6. It is worth noting two complicating factors about these figures: (1) it would have been difficult to gather accurate data regarding foreign populations in England for the same reasons it is difficult to keep track of the mobile and ghettoized homeless population in the late twentieth-century United States; (2) the term "Chinaman" was often used generically in reference to any Oriental, and this lack of differentiation is probably perpetuated in the census figures. But, regardless of their questionable accuracy with respect to details, the census figures indicated and/or helped to induce a popular consciousness of a growing Oriental population and a sense (correct or incorrect) of the predominantly Chinese origin of that population. Somewhat ironically, closer tabs were kept on Chinese immigrants to British colonies during the same period. An article in the *Times* of September 7, 1866, for instance, gives detailed figures regarding "the number of immigrants who left China for British Guiana, Trinidad, and Honduras" ("Chinese Emigration").
6. For accounts of the conditions in the United States, Australia, and New Zealand, see Musto, *The American Disease*, chap. 1; Walker, *Opium and Foreign Policy*, chap. 1; and a somewhat conspiracy-theory-oriented account by Szasz, *Ceremonial Chemistry*, chap. 6.
7. George Augustus Sala asks, "are we really in danger of being invaded by the 'Hea-

then Chinee,' not in his hundreds, but in his tens of thousands? Are our carpenters and plasterers, our stonemasons and bricklayers, nay our very navvies and gas-stokers, to be ruined by the competition of Chinese cheap labour? Are Betsy Jane the cook and Sarah Ann the housemaid to be ousted by the yellow men with the pig-tails, who cook so cleverly, make beds so neatly, and scrub floors so conscientiously; while Mrs. Tearall, the washerwoman, is elbowed from her tub by Ah Sing, the laundryman from Canton?" He concludes that "on the whole, it would be best if Ah Sing and his friends kept away from the land of the 'red-headed foreign devils'" (Sala, *Living London*, 425–26).

8. For a more detailed discussion of the role of the steamship in colonial expansion see Headrick, "The Tools of Imperialism," 235–39.

9. May, "The Chinese in Britain," 111.

10. Said, *Orientalism*, 26.

11. In one account, for instance, "the horse's head is turned—east" as "we leave familiar London" to enter "savage London," and the East Enders are equated with East globers: "the natives . . . will look upon us as the Japanese looked upon the first European travellers in the streets of Jeddo" (Doré and Jerrold, *London*, 142, 144).

12. The East End opium den and the evil Oriental underground were to become mainstays of post–World War I crime fiction, such as the mystery novels of Agatha Christie and Dorothy Sayers, and Sax Rohmer's stories of "the Chinese Moriarty," Fu Manchu (see Parssinen, *Secret Passions*, 115–26).

13. Wellesley, *Recollections*, 9.

14. Popular British myth places the origins of opium smoking in China, though there is no hard evidence to support such a hypothesis. An 1845 magazine article spins an elaborate fable of the Chinese origins of opium smoking with the story of Hingpoo, who started a kitchen fire with dried poppy stalks only to find that everyone in the kitchen became either sleepy or euphoric ("The Opium Smoker," 66–67).

15. "Lazarus," 421. The narrator's choice of nickname suggests anxieties he does not express directly. Lazarus, the leprotic beggar in Luke 16: 19–30 who was refused alms by the rich man Dives, turns the tables when he is in Heaven and Dives in Hell as he denies the rich man's pleas for water. The original Lazarus's leprosy lends the name overtones of contagion, and the cosmic revenge scenario suggests a teleological tipping of the class scales in favor of beggars, a shift that would put the "squalid and contemptible" Chinese beggar in a position of power over the Englishman who writes about him. The parable of Dives and Lazarus became something of a trope for Victorian middle-class anxieties about revolution, perhaps most notably in Elizabeth Gaskell's *Mary Barton* (1848), where it recurrently figures as the consolation of the Chartist John Barton who ultimately assassinates the local mill owner's son as part of a revolutionary scheme. It seems more than merely coincidental, one might add, that Barton is also an opium addict.

16. "Lazarus," 421–22. This suspicion of beggars was common in nineteenth-century England. As Jaffe argues, "Potentially productive individuals not engaged in productive labor . . . not only offended the age's emphasis on energy and productivity, but they also presented the Victorians with a constant threat of social unrest" (Jaffe, "Detecting the Beggar," 100). Mr. Policeman's scenario adds to this the fact that the offending nonworker is a foreigner and is presumably taking advantage of English

people who do work, waylaying hard-earned British money to finance his indulgence in shady foreign vices.

17. "Lazarus," 423.

18. Ibid.

19. "Opium Smoking in the East End," 177.

20. "Lazarus," 422.

21. "Opium Smoking in the East End," 175–76.

22. "Lazarus," 423–24.

23. "Opium Smoking in the East End," 177. Yet another account describes the extent of Lascar Sal's addiction: "Three halfpenny-worth only gives you a few minutes' smoke, and these men [three Chinese sailors] say they don't smoke more at a time. Lascar Sall [sic], a rather disreputable female, well known in the neighbourhood, would, they told me, smoke five shillings-worth of opium a day" (Ritchie, "In an Opium Den," 179).

24. Rowe, *Picked Up in the Streets,* 39.

25. "East London Opium Smokers," 72.

26. "Lazarus," 424.

27. Greenwood, "An Opium Smoke," 233.

28. "Shah's Visit."

29. "Wonderful Shah."

30. The trope recurs again and again in the shah ballads. Says another, "Now though one wife I am sure, / Is quite enough for most here, / He has not less than fifty score, / I mean the shah of Persia" ("Did You See the Shah"). For an extended discussion of the image of the Oriental man as sexual athlete in Victorian culture, see Marcus's chapter, "The Lustful Turk."

31. "Have You Seen the Shah."

32. See, for instance, Stevenson, who elaborates this very scenario ("A Vampire in the Mirror"), and Arata, who argues that the Transylvanian count is a figure not just of a threatening foreigner but specifically of a colonizing warrior from the East ("The Occidental Tourist").

33. Quoted in Stevenson, "A Vampire in the Mirror," 140.

34. Nead, *Myths of Sexuality,* 24, 33.

35. Poovey, *The Proper Lady,* 10.

36. Quoted in Nead, *Myths of Sexuality,* 33.

37. One such maternal representation of the British Empire was an allegorical anti-opium tract entitled *The Lady Britannia, Her Children, Her Step-children and Her Neighbours* (1892), the plot of which is summarized by Berridge and Edwards: "Lady Britannia, 'a loving mother', had found that many of her children had a fancy for opium, 'which she evidently thinks injurious, for she takes pains to prevent them from obtaining it. Anyone who sells it to them without its being labelled "Poison", meets with her severe condemnation.' With her step-children however, it was different. 'They had been badly brought up before she took them in hand; she now sends them tutors and Governors . . . and is in many respects a model step-mother . . . It certainly is a strange thing, if she had any love for them, that she should let them buy this opium to their hearts content'" (Berridge and Edwards, *Opium and the People,* 190). While the story criticizes Britain's opium policy, it nonetheless sees

the other machinery of empire (sending "tutors and Governors," and so on) as consistent with the acts of a loving "step-mother."

38. Garwood, *Our Plague Spot,* 95–97.
39. *Contagious Diseases.*
40. Fowle, "Aholah and Aholibah," 12–13.
41. "East London Opium Smokers," 68.
42. "A Night," 78–79.
43. Greenwood, "A Tamed Dragon," 102. Such predatory imagery is common in accounts like this. See, for instance, Greenwood's "Down Ratcliff Way" and "An Opium Smoke in Tiger Bay" and Ritchie's "Ratcliffe-Highway."
44. All references to *The Mystery of Edwin Drood* are cited parenthetically in the text by page number of Arthur J. Cox's edition.
45. Amanda Anderson discusses a similar impulse in Dickens's representations of "the fallen woman," who "herself becomes menacing . . . insofar as she metaleptically comes to figure those forces that determine her. In a rhetorical mimicry of the contagion so commonly attributed to tainted women, metalepsis transforms the fallen woman from a victim into a threat, an effect into a cause" (Amanda Anderson, *Tainted Souls,* 67). Though sexual fallenness is not emphasized in Princess Puffer's case, she nonetheless conforms to patterns similar to those Anderson describes as instances of "the Victorian cultural practice that wards off perceived predicaments of agency by displacing them onto a sexualized feminine figure" (ibid., 107).
46. Nead, *Myths of Sexuality,* 26.
47. Armstrong, *Desire and Domestic Fiction,* 60.
48. Other examples include the relationships between Little Nell and her Grandfather *(The Old Curiosity Shop),* David Copperfield and Mr. Micawber *(David Copperfield),* Mrs. Pocket and her brood *(Great Expectations),* and Mrs. Jellyby and her daughter *(Bleak House).* Many of these relationships acquire their parent-child overtones merely from the relative ages of the parties and do not involve biological families at all. They in fact call into question the very definitions of family relationships and thus also call into question the ideological work that the notion of the family has been made to do in Victorian English society—including the kind of self-serving work that is reflected in Princess Puffer's exploitation of the notion of maternity, and its parallel in the imperial model of Lady Britannia, her children, and step-children (see n. 37 above).
49. Victoria's image as the ideal domestic woman significantly contributed to her popularity. As one prominent clergyman preached of her, "one of her highest titles to our confidence and affection is found in her own domestic virtues. She is a *Queen*— a real *Queen*—but she is a real *Mother,* and a true *Wife*" (Rev. George S. Bull, quoted in Hall, "Sweet Delights," 50). That she was commonly known as "the 'Rosebud of England'" (ibid.) suggests that the character of Rosebud in *Edwin Drood* is also a comment on the same ideals of femininity attributed to the queen.
50. The two alternative names are discussed in Arthur J. Cox's n. 4 to chapter 22 of his Penguin edition of *Edwin Drood.*
51. "Lazarus," 424.
52. "East London Opium Smokers," 68.
53. Ibid.
54. The rumor that royalty and aristocracy had visited opium dens was persistent: "The

place is patronised, besides, by many distinguished members of the nobility and aristocracy of Great Britain," says another correspondent, "and it is rumoured even that Royalty itself has condescended to visit the opium master in his modest retreat" (Greenwood, "An Opium Smoke," 229). As late as 1895, the rumor of Prince Edward's visit persists, as recounted in "Chinese London and Its Opium Dens," 275.

55. Although Mother Abdallah "does the honours" in "Lazarus, Lotus-Eating," she does not do so professionally and emphasizes that "I don't pretend to make it as well as [Yahee] does" ("Lazarus," 423). Far from demystifying and challenging the Chinese master's exclusive power, she instead further mystifies and bolsters it.

56. Princess Puffer's tactic of remaining sober while her male customer is inebriated echoes the conventional means by which the prostitute "tigresses" are portrayed as securing power over "Jack Tar," the generic sailor. J. Ewing Ritchie describes the ruse: "There were public houses here [in Ratcliff Highway] . . . to which was attached a crew of infamous women; these bring Jack into the house to treat them, but while Jack drinks gin the landlord gives them from another tap water, and then against their sober villainy poor Jack has no chance" (Ritchie, "Ratcliffe-Highway," 83). The parallel will be explored at more length in chapter 6.

Chapter 6

1. This overlap of the foreign and the domestic is also an instance of what Brantlinger calls "the relation between imperialist adventure fiction and the seemingly more serious tradition of domestic realism." "These apparently antithetical genres do not have separate histories," he says, "but influence and shade into one another in countless ways from the Renaissance onward" (Brantlinger, *Rule of Darkness*, 13). This is also the essence of Bivona's thesis in *Desire and Contradiction* and explains an important aspect of what goes on especially in Conan Doyle's "The Man With the Twisted Lip," where, as we shall see, the domestic scene registers the cultural blending taking place at the levels of both the distant colonies and the nearby hearthside.

2. Jasper's opium vision is clearly a rehash of Coleridge and De Quincey's threatening Oriental dreams. The fearsome hordes of violent Orientals and the sense of vastness in general owe much to the earlier writers' visions, and the specters similarly betray an implicit fear of an invading Orient given access to the English consciousness through opium. De Quincey's shadow looms over *Edwin Drood* elsewhere as well, as in Canon Crisparkle's complaint that Mr. Honeythunder and his insidious tribe of rhetorically violent "philanthropists" are prone to "run amuck like so many mad Malays" (207).

3. This obvious clue has been taken up by other critics, such as T. W. Hill, who agrees that "the addition of some drug or sleeping mixture is plainly hinted" (Hill, "Notes," 203). Convention, as well as the other details of the plot, would argue for opium.

4. For an overview of narratives of the event—still a popular genre even after the turn of the century—see Brantlinger, *Rule of Darkness*, chap. 7.

5. Dickens, *Heart*, 350–51. See also the story he co-authored with Wilkie Collins for the 1857 Christmas number of *Household Words*, "The Perils of Certain English Prisoners," which presents a thinly masked recasting of the Mutiny and vents a great deal of indignation on the "Sambo," Christian George King.

6. It is tempting to see Neville as a sort of ventriloquist's dummy mouthing the senti-

ments appropriate to his author's idea of a "secret and revengeful" Oriental. Read in this light, Dickens's portrayal of Neville Landless seems consistent with Said's assertion that "it is Europe that articulates the Orient; this articulation is the prerogative, not of the puppet master, but of a genuine creator, whose life-giving power represents, animates, constitutes the otherwise silent and dangerous space beyond familiar boundaries" (Said, *Orientalism,* 57).

7. Catlike Indians inevitably suggest tigers, for the tiger had been popularly equated in England with a ferocious India at least since the 1790s with the anti-English exploits of Tipu Sultan, whose name means tiger in his native tongue, and who surrounded himself in his court at Seringapatam with tiger motifs ranging from tiger-embossed thrones to actual live tigers in his gardens. But even before that, abridged translations of Buffon's *Natural History* had rendered the tiger a symbol of unrestrained Oriental violence. He was possessed, said Buffon, by "an uniform rage, a blind fury; so blind, indeed, so undistinguishing, that not unoften he devours his own progeny, and if she offers to defend them, tears in pieces the dam herself.—Would that this thirst for his own blood the tiger gratified to an excess! Would that, by destroying them at their birth, he could extinguish the whole race of monsters which he produces!" (quoted in Barrell, *The Infection,* 49).

8. This is the same kind of contagion through physical proximity and social contact implied by Macaulay's assessment of Clive's questionable ethics in India: "this man, in all other parts of his life an honourable English gentleman and soldier, was no sooner matched against an Indian intriguer, and descended, without scruple, to falsehood, to hypocritical caresses, to the substitution of documents, and to the counterfeiting of hands" (quoted in Brantlinger, *Rule of Darkness,* 80). It is also strongly reminiscent of the acquired hybridity associated with Franklin Blake in *The Moonstone.*

9. Howard Duffield claims that Jasper is a member of the Hindu devotees of Kali, the Thuggees, and that he assassinates Edwin in accordance with that sect's secret rituals (Duffield, "John Jasper"). Aylmer similarly speculates that Jasper is born of an Egyptian mother, and that his supposed murder of Edwin is part of a complicated scheme of revenge in an Egyptian blood feud (Aylmer, *The Drood Case*). The scenario has become so familiar that Suvendrini Perera takes it as an unspoken presupposition for her reading of the novel (Perera, *Reaches of Empire*).

10. Duffield, "John Jasper—Strangler," 582.

11. Many of the opium den narratives written after *Edwin Drood* use conventions clearly established by Dickens and even attribute their inspiration explicitly to him. Representative of this trend is an article that appeared in the pharmaceutical trade journal *Chemist and Druggist* shortly after Dickens's death. Says the author, "The description of the opium den in the first and last parts of 'The Mystery of Edwin Drood,' has aroused such general interest that I have ventured to write out my notes of a visit to the very same chamber (as I have reason to believe) wherein are enacted the gloomily picturesque scenes related in those pages" ("Opium Smoking in Bluegate Fields," 259).

12. Bivona, *Desire and Contradiction,* 35. Dressing up as an East Ender is an essential part of the slumming expedition in several opium den narratives. See, for instance, "Opium Smoking in Bluegate Fields," 259; Doré and Jerrold, *London: A Pilgrimage,*

142; Greenwood, "An Opium Smoke," 229; as well as Wilde and Conan Doyle (discussed below).

13. The narrators never mention smoking opium themselves in the accounts published before *Edwin Drood,* but personal experience of smoking is an integral part of the accounts published afterward (see, for instance, "Opium Smoking in Bluegate Fields," "Chinese London and Its Opium Dens," "A Night in an Opium Den," and Greenwood, "An Opium Smoke in Tiger Bay"). Although the one firsthand account of Dickens's visit to an opium den does not mention his smoking there, it does intimate that he had been there more than once before (Fields, *Yesterdays with Authors,* 202–3), and a subsequent explorer even finds witnesses who claim to remember a man matching Dickens's description smoking there, though they cannot swear that he visited before Dickens's death ("Opium Smoking in Bluegate Fields," 261).

14. All references in the text to *The Picture of Dorian Gray* are cited parenthetically by page number of Peter Ackroyd's edition.

In this particular habit Lord Henry appears to be modeled after his author. As Marcel Schwob said of Wilde during the year he composed *Dorian Gray,* "he never stopped smoking opium-tainted Egyptian cigarettes" (quoted in Ellmann, *Oscar Wilde,* 346). Opium-tainted cigarettes in particular had already been targeted by the anti-opium press as one of the more insidious ways to disseminate the destructive influence of opium smoke beyond the opium den: "The last device for secretly supplying the slaves of opium in San Francisco is said to be a tiny cigar made from tobacco which has been impregnated with the fumes of the burning drug. The poison is more effectually administered in this manner than when the smoke is inhaled directly from the burning paste" ("Opium Cigarettes," 208).

15. Because opium was the most common home remedy for a number of common ailments for much of the century, it would not have been unusual to find it in a middle-class home. But it would almost certainly have been in the form of either laudanum or one of the many patent remedies (see chapter 1), and even these would not likely have been found in the library, nor would they have been guiltily hidden. The pasty-waxy raw opium Wilde describes was at that time sold exclusively to chemists and druggists, having been forbidden to others by the Pharmacy Act of 1868. It is possible that Wilde meant to evoke another stereotypically Oriental consciousness-altering substance, hashish, which appears in the Orientalist prose of his beloved Nerval as "a box full of a greenish paste" (Nerval, *Journey to the Orient,* 87). "Waxy," however, is an adjective consistently associated with opium, and never explicitly with hashish. Even if Dorian's box is filled with hashish rather than opium, though, the implications of Oriental infringement upon, and increasing possession of, middle-class environments beyond the East End are much the same.

16. Eric Meyer argues that "as European colonization of the East in the eighteenth and nineteenth centuries increased the amount of intercourse between radically different cultures and races, . . . monstrosity . . . came to signify an ethnographic transgression of the firm lines of distinction between 'races,' as enacted in miscegenation that resulted in 'monstrous' hybrids of indeterminate racial/cultural origins" (Meyer, "I Know Thee Not," 695).

17. Conan Doyle was there at the birth of *Dorian Gray* in September of 1889 when he

and Wilde attended a dinner given by J. M. Stoddart, editor of *Lippincott's,* and both authors left the table with contracts to produce stories for the popular monthly. Wilde's contribution was the preliminary version of *The Picture of Dorian Gray,* and Conan Doyle submitted his second Sherlock Holmes novel, *The Sign of Four.* The original magazine version of *Dorian Gray* did not include the visit to the opium den, which first appeared in the book published by Ward, Lock, and Company in April 1891 (Ellmann, *Oscar Wilde,* 313, 322–23), but Conan Doyle admired Wilde and almost surely read both versions of *Dorian Gray* before producing "The Man With the Twisted Lip" for *Strand Magazine* the following December.

18. All references in the text to "The Man With the Twisted Lip" are cited parenthetically by page number of its first publication in the *Strand Magazine* of 1891.

19. Audrey Jaffe explores something like a contagion anxiety around class identity in the story, claiming that both the beggar and the capitalist "man who does something in the City" are anathema to a nineteenth-century work ethic because both are able to earn a living without apparently putting in an honest day's work. She argues that it is this invisible mode of production, both liberating and anxiety-inducing, that dissolves the distinction between St. Clair and the beggar Hugh Boone: neither identity has a visible basis, both being paradoxically grounded in exchange (Jaffe, "Detecting the Beggar").

20. Similar descriptions abound. A typical instance is Richard Rowe's description of "Johnson the Chinaman": "When the light falls on his filmy-eyed, twitching, sickly-yellow face, it looks not unlike that of a galvanised corpse" (Rowe, *Picked Up in the Streets,* 42).

21. The anti-opium *Friend of China* sometimes reprinted accounts of other experiments like Whitney's. In one of them, two medical students mix opium with their tobacco and are later found lying almost dead in the street ("The Danger"). The same kind of seepage beyond the opium den is implicit in Lord Henry Wotton's and his author's opium-tainted cigarettes and the *Friend of China's* warning against them ("Opium Cigarettes").

22. For an accessible overview of these phenomena, see Hapgood, "Viruses Emerge."

23. The surfacing of such delayed complications became a theme in early twentieth-century British fiction, movies, and popular journalism, all of which portrayed vast Oriental criminal undergrounds only occasionally visible to the average observer but supposedly controlling and degrading British culture primarily by means of opiates and cocaine. For an overview see Parssinen's chapter "Agents of Corruption" (Parssinen, *Secret Passions,* 115–28).

24. The notion that opiates permanently alter and take control of the user's cells becomes a standard trope in the literature of opiate addiction. William S. Burroughs is a representative example: "I think the use of junk causes permanent cellular alteration. Once a junky, always a junky. You can stop using junk, but you are never off after the first habit" (Burroughs, *Junky,* 117).

Works Cited

Abrams, M. H. *The Milk of Paradise: The Effects of Opium Visions on the Works of De Quincey, Crabbe, Francis Thompson, and Coleridge.* Cambridge: Harvard Univ. Press, 1934.

Alcock, Rutherford. "Sir Rutherford Alcock's Paper." In *All About Opium.* Ed. Hartmann Henry Sultzberger. London: Wertheimer, Lea, 1884. 27–66.

Altick, Richard D. *Victorian People and Ideas.* New York: Norton, 1973.

Anderson, Amanda. *Tainted Souls and Painted Faces: The Rhetoric of Fallenness in Victorian Culture.* Ithaca, N.Y.: Cornell Univ. Press, 1993.

Anderson, Benedict. *Imagined Communities: Reflections on the Origin and Spread of Nationalism.* Rev. ed. London: Verso, 1991.

Arata, Stephen D. "The Occidental Tourist: *Dracula* and the Anxiety of Reverse Colonization." *Victorian Studies* 33 (1989–90): 621–45.

Archer, Mildred. *Tippoo's Tiger.* London: Her Majesty's Stationery Office, 1959.

Arendt, Hannah. *The Origins of Totalitarianism.* New ed. New York: Harcourt Brace Jovanovich, 1973.

Armstrong, Nancy. *Desire and Domestic Fiction: A Political History of the Novel.* Oxford: Oxford Univ. Press, 1987.

Aylmer, Felix. *The Drood Case.* London: Rupert Hart-Davis, 1964.

Barrell, John. *The Infection of Thomas De Quincey: A Psychopathology of Imperialism.* New Haven: Yale Univ. Press, 1991.

Baudelaire, Charles. "from 'The Poem of Hashish.'" Trans. Andrew C. Kimmens. In *The Drug User: Documents, 1840–1960.* Ed. John Strausbaugh and Donald Blaise. New York: Blast Books, 1991. 36–49.

Baumgart, Winfried. *Imperialism: The Idea and Reality of British and French Colonial Expansion, 1880–1914.* Oxford: Oxford Univ. Press, 1982.

Beer, J. B., *Coleridge the Visionary.* London: Chatto and Windus, 1959.

Berridge, Virginia. "East End Opium Dens and Narcotic Use in Britain." *London Journal* 4 (1978): 3–28.

———, and Griffith Edwards. *Opium and the People: Opiate Use in Nineteenth-Century England.* 1981. New Haven: Yale Univ. Press: 1987.

Bhabha, Homi K. "The Other Question . . . : Homi K. Bhabha Reconsiders the Stereotype and Colonial Discourse." *Screen* 24 (November-December 1983): 18–36.

———. "Signs Taken for Wonders: Questions of Ambivalence and Authority Under a Tree Outside Delhi, May 1817." In *"Race," Writing, and Difference.* Ed. Henry Louis Gates, Jr. Chicago: Univ. of Chicago Press, 1986. 163–84.

Bivona, Daniel. *Desire and Contradiction: Imperial Visions and Domestic Debates in Victorian Literature*. Manchester and New York: Manchester Univ. Press, 1990.

Blair, William. "from 'An Opium Eater in America.'" In *The Drug User: Documents, 1840–1960*. Ed. John Strausbaugh and Donald Blaise. New York: Blast Books, 1991. 185–89.

Bodkin, Maud. *Archetypal Patterns in Poetry: Psychological Studies of the Imagination*. 1934. New York: Vintage, 1958.

Brantlinger, Patrick. *Rule of Darkness: British Literature and Imperialism, 1830–1914*. Ithaca, N.Y.: Cornell Univ. Press, 1988.

Brennan, Timothy. "The National Longing for Form." In *Nation and Narration*. Ed. Homi K. Bhabha. London: Routledge, 1990. 44–70.

Brontë, Anne. *The Tenant of Wildfell Hall*. 1848. Ed. G. D. Hargreaves. Harmondsworth, England: Penguin, 1979.

Bruss, Elizabeth W. *Autobiographical Acts: The Changing Situation of a Literary Genre*. Baltimore: Johns Hopkins Univ. Press, 1976.

Burroughs, William S. *Junky*. 1953. Harmondsworth, England: Penguin, 1977.

Chaudhouri, Nupur. "Memsahibs and Motherhood in Nineteenth-Century Colonial India." *Victorian Studies* 31 (1987–88): 517–35.

Cheyfitz, Eric. *The Poetics of Imperialism: Translation and Colonization from The Tempest to Tarzan*. Oxford: Oxford Univ. Press, 1991.

"Chinese Emigration." *Times*, Sept. 7, 1866, 8.

"Chinese London and Its Opium Dens." *Gentlemen's Magazine* 279 (1895): 273–82.

Choo, Ng Kwee. *The Chinese in London*. Oxford: Oxford Univ. Press, 1968.

Clifford, James. *The Predicament of Culture: Twentieth-Century Ethnography, Literature, and Art*. Cambridge: Harvard Univ. Press, 1988.

Coleridge, Samuel Taylor. *Collected Letters of Samuel Taylor Coleridge*. Ed. Earl Leslie Griggs. 6 vols. Oxford: Clarendon Press, 1956–71.

———. *Complete Poetical Works*. Ed. Ernest Hartley Coleridge. 2 vols. Oxford: Oxford Univ. Press, 1912.

———. "Crewe MS of 'Kubla Khan.'" In *William Wordsworth and the Age of English Romanticism*. Ed. Jonathan Wordsworth, Michael C. Jaye, and Robert Woof. New Brunswick, N.J.: Rutgers Univ. Press, 1987. 184–85.

———. "Lectures on Revealed Religion, Lecture 6." In *The Collected Works of Samuel Taylor Coleridge*. 16 vols. London: Routledge and Kegan Paul, 1969–73. 1: 215–29.

———. *The Notebooks of Samuel Taylor Coleridge*. Ed. Kathleen Coburn. 5 vols. New York: Pantheon, 1957.

Colley, Linda. "Whose Nation? Class and National Consciousness in Britain, 1750–1830." *Past and Present* 113 (1986): 97–117.

Collins, Wilkie. *The Moonstone*. 1868. Ed. J. I. M. Stewart. Harmondsworth, England: Penguin, 1966.

———. "A Sermon for Sepoys." *Household Words* 17 (Dec. 19, 1857–June 12, 1858): 244–47.

[———, and Charles Dickens]. "The Perils of Certain English Prisoners." *Household Words* Christmas Number 1857 (Dec. 7, 1857).

Collis, Maurice. *Foreign Mud: being an account of the Opium Imbroglio at Canton in the 1830's and the Anglo-Chinese War That Followed.* London: Faber and Faber, 1946.

Conan Doyle, Arthur. "The Man With the Twisted Lip." *Strand Magazine* (1891): 623–37.

Contagious Diseases. A Bill For the Prevention of Contagious Diseases at certain Naval and Military Stations. Bill 163. London: House of Commons, 1864.

Cottrell, Stella. "The Devil on Two Sticks: Franco-phobia in 1803." In *Patriotism: The Making and Unmaking of British National Identity.* Ed. Raphael Samuel. 3 vols. London: Routledge, 1989. 1:259–74.

Courtwright, David T. *Dark Paradise: Opiate Addiction in America Before 1940.* Cambridge: Harvard Univ. Press, 1982.

Crompton, Louis. *Byron and Greek Love: Homophobia in Nineteenth-Century England.* Berkeley, Calif.: Univ. of California Press, 1985.

"The Danger of Experimenting in Opium-Smoking." *Friend of China* 6 (1883): 95–96.

Davidson, Miriam. "Can Soldiers Stop Drugs?: Militarizing the Mexican Border." *The Nation* 252 (1991): 406–10.

Davis, Nuel Pharr. *The Life of Wilkie Collins.* Urbana: Univ. of Illinois, 1956.

de Mas, Sinibaldo. "Translation of Don Sinibaldo's Chapter." In *All About Opium.* Ed. Hartmann Henry Sultzberger. London: Wertheimer, Lea, 1884. 86–95.

Densmore, John. *Riders on the Storm: My Life With Jim Morrison and the Doors.* New York: Doubleday, 1990.

De Quincey, Thomas. "Autobiography from 1785 to 1803." *Collected Writings* 1.

——. "Canton Expedition and Convention." *Blackwood's* 50 (1841): 677–88.

——. "The Casuistry of Roman Meals." *Collected Writings* 7:11–43.

——. *The Collected Writings of Thomas De Quincey.* Ed. David Masson. 14 vols. London: A. and C. Black, 1896–97.

——. *Confessions of an English Opium Eater.* 1821. Ed. Alethea Hayter. Harmondsworth, England: Penguin, 1971.

——. "Confessions of an English Opium-Eater: Author's Revised and Enlarged Version of 1856." *Collected Writings* 3:209–449.

——. "The English Mail-Coach." *Collected Writings* 13:270–330.

——. "Kant on National Character in Relation to the Sense of the Sublime and Beautiful: A Translation." *Collected Writings* 14:46–60.

——. "On Murder Considered as One of the Fine Arts." *Collected Writings* 13:9–124.

——. "Suspiria De Profundis, Being a Sequel to 'The Confessions of an English Opium-Eater.'" *Collected Writings* 13:331–69.

——. "System of the Heavens As Revealed by Lord Rosse's Telescopes." In *Collected Writings* 8:7–34.

Dickens, Charles. *The Heart of Charles Dickens as Revealed in His Letters to Angela Burdett-Coutts.* Ed. Edgar Johnson. New York and Boston: Duell, Sloan and Pearce-Little, Brown, 1952.

——. *The Mystery of Edwin Drood.* 1870. Ed. Arthur J. Cox. Harmondsworth, England: Penguin, 1974.

"Did You See the Shah." London: Disley, n.d.

Doré, Gustave and Blanchard Jerrold. *London: A Pilgrimage*. 1872. New York: Benjamin Blom, 1968.

Douglas, Mary. *Purity and Danger: An Analysis of Concepts of Pollution and Taboo*. New York: Praeger, 1966.

Drew, John. "Coleridge, 'Kubla Khan,' and the Rise of Tantric Buddhism." In *India and the Romantic Imagination*. Oxford: Oxford Univ. Press, 1987.

Duffield, Howard. "John Jasper—Strangler." *The Bookman* (1930): 581–88.

"East London Opium Smokers." *London Society* 14 (1868): 68–72.

Eliot, George. *Middlemarch*. 1872. Ed. W. J. Harvey. Harmondsworth, England: Penguin, 1965.

Ellmann, Richard. *Oscar Wilde*. New York: Alfred A. Knopf, 1988.

"Every Agent's a Drug Agent: The War on the Border." *Newsweek*, May 1, 1989, 27.

Fields, James T. *Yesterdays With Authors*. Boston: Houghton, Mifflin and Co., 1898.

Fildes, Valerie. *Wet Nursing: A History from Antiquity to the Present*. Oxford: Basil Blackwell, 1988.

Forrest, Denys. *Tiger of Mysore: The Life and Death of Tipu Sultan*. London: Chatto and Windus, 1970.

Fowle, Fulwar William. "Aholah and Aholibah. A Sermon, Having Reference to Recent Immoral Legislation by the British Parliament. Preached in the Cathedral Town of Salisbury 4th Sunday After Trinity, 1871. By the Rev. Fulwar William Fowle, M.A., Prebendary of Chisenbury and Chute." London: Tweedie and Co., 1871.

Freud, Sigmund. "Beyond the Pleasure Principle." In *The Standard Edition of the Complete Psychological Works of Sigmund Freud*. Trans. and ed. James Strachey. 24 vols. London: Hogarth Press, 1953–74. 18:7–64.

Gagnier, Regenia. *Subjectivities: A History of Self-Representation in Britain, 1832–1920*. Oxford: Oxford Univ. Press, 1991.

Gardner, Brian. *The East India Company*. London: Rupert Hart-Davis, 1971.

Garwood, John. *Our Plague Spot: In Connection With Our Polity and Usages, as Regards Our Women, Our Soldiery, and the Indian Empire*. London: Thomas Cautley Newby, 1859.

Gaskell, Elizabeth. *Mary Barton: A Tale of Manchester Life*. 1848. Ed. Stephen Gill. Harmondsworth, England: Penguin, 1970.

Green, Martin. *Dreams of Adventure, Deeds of Empire*. New York: Basic Books, 1979.

Greenwood, James. "Down Ratcliff Way." In *Low-Life Deeps: An Account of the Strange Fish to be Found There*. London: Chatto and Windus, 1876. 115–27.

——. "A Tamed Dragon." In *Mysteries of Modern London. By One of the Crowd*. London: Diprose and Bateman, n.d. 100–7.

——. "An Opium Smoke in Tiger Bay." In *In Strange Company: Being the Experiences of a Roving Correspondent*. London: Henry S. King and Co., 1873. 229–38.

Hall, Catherine. "Missionary Stories: Gender and Ethnicity in England in the 1830s and 1840s." In *Cultural Studies*. Ed. Lawrence Grossberg, Cary Nelson, and Paula A. Treichler. New York: Routledge, 1992.

——. "The Sweet Delights of Home." In *A History of Private Life IV: From the Fires of Revolution to the Great War*. Ed. Michelle Perrot. Trans. Arthur Goldhammer. Cambridge: Belknap-Harvard Univ. Press, 1990.

Hapgood, Fred. "Viruses Emerge as a New Key for Unlocking Life's Mysteries." *Smithsonian* (November 1987): 117–127.

"Have You Seen the Shah." London: Disley, n.d.

Hayter, Alethea. *Opium and the Romantic Imagination.* 1968. Wellingborough: Crucible, 1988.

Headrick, Daniel R. "The Tools of Imperialism: Technology and the Expansion of European Colonial Empires in the Nineteenth Century." *Journal of Modern History* 51 (1979): 231–63.

Hill, T. W. "Notes on *The Mystery of Edwin Drood.*" *Dickensian* 40 (1944): 198–204; *Dickensian* 41 (1944–45): 30–37.

Hobsbawm, E. J. *Nations and Nationalism Since 1780: Programme, Myth, Reality.* Cambridge: Cambridge Univ. Press, 1990.

Hofmann, Albert. "from *LSD: My Problem Child.*" In *The Drug User: Documents, 1840–1960.* Ed. John Strausbaugh and Donald Blaise. New York: Blast Books, 1991. 80–92.

Holmes, Richard. *Coleridge: Early Visions.* London: Hodder and Stoughton, 1989.

Honour, Hugh. "The Vision of Cathay." In *Chinoiserie.* London: John Murray, 1961.

Hook, Theodore. *The Life of General, the Right Honourable Sir David Baird, Bart. G.C.B K.C., &c. &c.* Rev. ed. 2 vols. London: Richard Bentley, 1833.

Huxley, Aldous. "The Doors of Perception." In *"The Doors of Perception" and "Heaven and Hell."* New York: Harper and Row, 1963.

"In an Opium Den." *Ragged School Union Magazine* 20 (1868): 198–200.

Jaffe, Audrey. "Detecting the Beggar: Arthur Conan Doyle, Henry Mayhew, and 'The Man With the Twisted Lip.'" *Representations* 31 (Summer 1990): 96–117.

Kabbani, Rana. *Europe's Myths of Orient.* Bloomington: Indiana Univ. Press, 1986.

Kane, H. H. "A Hashish-House in New York." In *The Drug User: Documents, 1840–1960.* Ed. John Strausbaugh and Donald Blaise. New York: Blast Books, 1991. 164–72.

Latimer, Dean and Jeff Goldberg. *Flowers in the Blood: The Story of Opium.* New York: Franklin Watts, 1981.

"Lazarus Lotus-Eating." *All the Year Round* 15 (1866): 421–25.

Leask, Nigel. *British Romantic Writers and the East: Anxieties of Empire.* Cambridge: Cambridge Univ. Press, 1992.

——. "'Murdering One's Double': De Quincey's 'Confessions of an English Opium Eater' and S. T. Coleridge's 'Biographia Literaria.'" *Prose Studies* 13 (December 1990): 78–98.

Lefebure, Molly. *Samuel Taylor Coleridge: A Bondage of Opium.* New York: Stein and Day, 1974.

Lindop, Grevel. *The Opium-Eater: A Life of Thomas De Quincey.* London: J. M. Dent and Sons, 1981.

——. "Lamb, Hazlitt, and De Quincey." In *The Coleridge Connection: Essays for Thomas McFarland.* Ed. Richard Gravil and Molly Lefebure. New York: St. Martin's, 1990.

Lonoff, Sue. *Wilkie Collins and His Victorian Readers: A Study in the Rhetoric of Authorship.* New York: AMS, 1982.

Lovejoy, Arthur O. "The Chinese Origin of a Romanticism." In *Essays in the History of Ideas.* Baltimore: Johns Hopkins Univ. Press, 1948.

Lowe, Lisa. *Critical Terrains: French and British Orientalisms.* Ithaca, N.Y.: Cornell Univ. Press, 1991.

Lowes, John Livingston. *The Road to Xanadu: A Study in the Ways of the Imagination*. Boston: Houghton Mifflin, 1930.

Ludlow, Fitz Hugh. "from *The Hasheesh Eater: Being Passages From The Life of a Pythagorean*." In *The Drug User: Documents, 1840–1960*. Edited by John Strausbaugh and Donald Blaise. New York: Blast Books, 1991. 93–114.

"Major Drug Bust Nets 1,200 Pounds of Pure Heroin," *Raleigh (N.C.) News and Observer,* June 22, 1991, A3.

Marcus, Steven. "The Lustful Turk." In *The Other Victorians: A Study of Sexuality and Pornography in Mid-Nineteenth-Century England*. New York: Basic Books, 1964.

May, J. P. "The Chinese in Britain, 1860–1914." In *Immigrants and Minorities in British Society*. Ed. Colin Holmes. London: Allen and Unwin, 1978. 111–24.

Meyer, Eric. "'I Know Thee Not, I Loathe Thy Race': Romantic Orientalism in the Eye of the Other." *ELH* 58 (1991): 657–99.

Mezzrow, Milton "Mezz" and Bernard Wolfe. *Really the Blues*. New York: Random House, 1946.

Miller, D. A. *The Novel and the Police*. Berkeley, Calif.: Univ. of California Press, 1988.

Moore-Gilbert, B. J. *Kipling and "Orientalism."* New York: St. Martin's, 1986.

Morgan, H. Wayne. *Drugs in America: A Social History, 1800–1980*. Syracuse, N.Y.: Syracuse Univ. Press, 1981.

Musto, David F. *The American Disease: Origins of Narcotic Control*. Expanded ed. Oxford: Oxford Univ. Press, 1987.

———. "Opium, Cocaine and Marijuana in American History." *Scientific American* 265 (July 1991): 40–47.

Nead, Lynda. *Myths of Sexuality: Representations of Women in Victorian Britain*. Cambridge, England: Basil Blackwell, 1988.

de Nerval, Gerard. *Journey to the Orient*. Trans. and ed. Norman Glass. New York: New York Univ. Press, 1972.

New Large-Scale Ordnance Atlas of London and Suburbs with Supplementary Maps, Copious Letterpress Descriptions and Alphabetical Indexes. London: George W. Bacon, 1888.

Newman, Charles. *The Evolution of Medical Education in the Nineteenth Century*. Oxford: Oxford Univ. Press, 1957.

Newman, F. W. "Address, by Emer. 'Prof.' F.W. Newman, to the London Conference, 5th May, 1870, Against the Contagious Diseases Act, On the Topic Assigned to Him." Nottingham: National Anti-Contagious Disease Acts Assoc., 1870.

"A Night in an Opium Den." *Strand Magazine* 1 (1891): 624–27.

Nin, Anaïs. "from *The Diary of Anaïs Nin, 1947–1955*." In *The Drug User: Documents, 1840–1960*. Edited by John Strausbaugh and Donald Blaise. New York: Blast Books, 1991. 142–47.

"Opium Cigarettes." *Friend of China* 6 (1883): 208.

"An Opium Den in Whitechapel." *Chemist and Druggist* 9 (1868): 275.

"The Opium Smoker." *Bentley's Miscellany* 17 (1845): 65–69.

"Opium Smoking at the East End of London." Reprinted from the *Daily News* of 1864. In *All About Opium*. Ed. Hartmann Henry Sultzberger. London: Wertheimer, Lea, 1884. 174–77.

"Opium Smoking in Bluegate Fields." *Chemist and Druggist* 11 (1870): 259–61.

Parssinen, Terry M. *Secret Passions, Secret Remedies: Narcotic Drugs in British Society, 1820–1930.* Philadelphia: Institute for the Study of Human Issues, 1983.

Paxton, Nancy L. "Mobilizing Chivalry: Rape in British Novels About the Indian Uprising of 1857." *Victorian Studies* 36 (1992–93): 5–30.

Pepper, Art and Laurie. *Straight Life: The Story of Art Pepper.* New York: Macmillan, 1979.

Perera, Suvendrini. *Reaches of Empire: The English Novel from Edgeworth to Dickens.* New York: Columbia Univ. Press, 1991.

Perry, Ruth. "Colonizing the Breast: Sexuality and Maternity in Eighteenth-Century England." *Journal of the History of Sexuality* 2 (1991–92): 204–34.

Philips, C. H. *The East India Company: 1784–1834.* Manchester: Manchester Univ. Press, 1961.

Piercy, George. "Opium Smoking in London." *Friend of China* 6 (1883): 239–40.

Poe, Edgar Allan. *The Complete Tales and Poems of Edgar Allan Poe.* New York: Modern Library, 1938.

Poovey, Mary. *The Proper Lady and the Woman Writer: Ideology as Style in the Works of Mary Wollstonecraft, Mary Shelley, and Jane Austen.* Chicago: Univ. of Chicago Press, 1984.

Punter, David. *The Romantic Unconscious: A Study in Narcissism and Patriarchy.* New York: New York Univ. Press, 1990.

Purchas, Samuel. *Purchas his Pilgrimage. Or Relations of the World and the Religions Observed in All Ages and Places Discovered.* . . . London: William Stansby, 1614.

Reed, John R. "English Imperialism and the Unacknowledged Crime of *The Moonstone*." *Clio* 2 (1972–73): 281–90.

Reynolds, Charles. *Modes of Imperialism.* New York: St. Martin's, 1981.

Ritchie, J. Ewing. "In an Opium Den." In *Days and Nights in London: Or, Studies in Black and Gray.* London: Tinsley Brothers, 1880. 170–81.

———. "Ratcliffe-Highway." In *The Night-Side of London.* London: William Tweedie, 1858. 75–84.

Roberts, Ann. "Mothers and babies: the wetnurse and her employer in mid-nineteenth-century England." *Women's Studies* 3 (1976): 279–93.

Robinson, Kenneth. *Wilkie Collins: A Biography.* London: Bodley Head, 1951.

Ross, Marlon B. "Romancing the Nation-State: The Poetics of Romantic Nationalism." In *Macropolitics of Nineteenth-Century Literature: Nationalism, Exoticism, Impressionism.* Ed. Jonathan Arac and Harriet Ritvo. Philadelphia: Univ. of Pennsylvania Press, 1991.

Rowe, Richard. *Picked Up in the Streets.* London: W. H. Allen, 1880.

Rycroft, Charles. *Imagination and Reality.* New York: International Univ. Press, 1968.

Said, Edward W. *Orientalism.* New York: Vintage, 1979.

Sala, George Augustus. *Living London: Being "Echoes" Re-echoed.* London: Remington, 1883.

Schneider, Elisabeth. *Coleridge, Opium and Kubla Khan.* Chicago: Univ. of Chicago Press, 1953.

Sedgwick, Eve Kosofsky. *Between Men: English Literature and Male Homosocial Desire.* New York: Columbia Univ. Press, 1985.

———. "Language as Live Burial: Thomas De Quincey." In *The Coherence of Gothic Conventions.* New York: Methuen, 1986. 37–96.

Seeley, J. R. *The Expansion of England.* 1883. Ed. John Gross. Chicago: Univ. of Chicago, 1971.

Shaffer, E. S. *"Kubla Kahn" and the Fall of Jerusalem: The Mythological School in Biblical Criticism and Secular Literature, 1770–1880.* Cambridge: Cambridge Univ. Press, 1975.

"The Shah's Visit to the Queen of England." London: Disley, n.d.

Siegel, Ronald K. *Intoxication: Life in Pursuit of Artificial Paradise.* New York: Dutton, 1989.

Spivak, Gayatri Chakravorty. "Can the Subaltern Speak?" In *Marxism and the Interpretation of Culture.* Ed. Cary Nelson and Lawrence Grossberg. Urbana: Univ. of Illinois Press, 1988. 271–313.

Stevens, Jay. *Storming Heaven: LSD and the American Dream.* New York: Harper and Row, 1988.

Stevenson, John Allen. "A Vampire in the Mirror: The Sexuality of *Dracula.*" *PMLA* 103 (1988): 139–149.

Suleri, Sara. *The Rhetoric of English India.* Chicago: Univ. of Chicago Press, 1992.

Szasz, Thomas. *Ceremonial Chemistry: The Ritual Persecution of Drugs, Addicts, and Pushers.* Holmes Beach: Learning Publications, 1985.

Tomlinson, John. *Cultural Imperialism: A Critical Introduction.* Baltimore: Johns Hopkins Univ. Press, 1991.

Towell, Pat, and John Felton. "Invasion, Noriega Ouster Win Support on Capitol Hill." *Congressional Quarterly Weekly Report* 47 (1989): 3532–35.

Turner, Storrs. "Letters from the Rev. Storrs Turner." In *All About Opium.* Ed. Hartmann Henry Sultzberger. London: Wertheimer, Lea, 1884. 96–97.

"A Visit to an Opium House." *Eclectic Magazine,* n.s., 8 (1868): 1379–85.

Visram, Rozina. *Ayahs, Lascars and Princes: Indians in Britain 1700–1947.* London: Pluto Press, 1986.

Viswanathan, Gauri. *Masks of Conquest: Literary Study and British Rule in India.* New York: Columbia Univ. Press, 1989.

Walker, William O., III. *Opium and Foreign Policy: The Anglo-American Search for Order in Asia, 1912–1954.* Chapel Hill: Univ. of North Carolina Press, 1991.

Watlington, Dennis. "Between the Cracks." *Vanity Fair,* December 1987, 146–51, 184–86.

Wellesley, Frederick. *Recollections of a Soldier-Diplomat.* London: Hutchinson and Co., n.d.

Wheeler, J. Talboys. *India of the Vedic Age with Reference to the Mahabharata.* Vol. 1 of *The History of India.* Delhi: Cosmo Publications, 1973.

——. *India of the Brahmanic Age With Reference to the Ramayana.* Vol. 2 of *The History of India.* 2 vols. Delhi: Cosmo Publications, 1973.

——. *India from the Earliest Ages: Hindu Buddhist and Brahmanical Revival.* Vol. 3 of *The History of India.* Delhi: Cosmo Publications, 1973.

——. *The History of India under Mussulman Rule.* Vol. 4 of *The History of India.* 2 vols. London: Trubner and Co., 1876.

Wilbur, Marguerite Eyer. *The East India Company and the British Empire in the Far East.* New York: Richard R. Smith, 1945.

Wilde, Oscar. *The Picture of Dorian Gray.* 1891. Ed. Peter Ackroyd. Harmondsworth, England: Penguin, 1985.

Witkiewicz, Stanislaw Ignacy. "Report About the Effects of Peyote on Stanislaw Ignacy Witkiewicz." In *The Drug User: Documents, 1840–1960.* Ed. John Strausbaugh and Donald Blaise. New York: Blast Books, 1991. 231–37.

"The Wonderful Shah of Persia" London: Disley, n.d.

Yapp, M. E. "'The Brightest Jewel': The Origins of a Phrase." In *East India Company Studies: Papers Presented to Professor Cyril Philips.* Ed. Kenneth Ballhatchet and John Harrison. Hong Kong: Asian Research Service. 31–67.

Index

VICTORIAN LITERATURE AND CULTURE SERIES

Karen Chase, Jerome J. McGann, *and* Herbert Tucker, *General Editors*

—◦◦◦◦∞◦◦◦—

DANIEL ALBRIGHT
Tennyson: *The Muses' Tug of War*

DAVID G. RIEDE
Matthew Arnold and the Betrayal of Language

ANTHONY WINNER
Culture and Irony: *Studies in Joseph Conrad's Major Novels*

JAMES RICHARDSON
Vanishing Lives: *Style and Self in Tennyson, D. G. Rossetti, Swinburne, and Yeats*

JEROME J. McGANN, EDITOR
Victorian Connections

ANTONY H. HARRISON
Victorian Poets and Romantic Poems: *Intertextuality and Ideology*

E. WARWICK SLINN
The Discourse of Self in Victorian Poetry

LINDA K. HUGHES AND MICHAEL LUND
The Victorian Serial

ANNA LEONOWENS
The Romance of the Harem
Edited and with an Introduction by Susan Morgan

ALAN FISCHLER
Modified Rapture: *Comedy in W. S. Gilbert's Savoy Operas*

BARBARA TIMM GATES, EDITOR
Journal of Emily Shore, with a new Introduction by the Editor

RICHARD MAXWELL
The Mysteries of Paris and London

FELICIA BONAPARTE
The Gypsy-Bachelor of Manchester: *The Life of Mrs. Gaskell's Demon*

PETER L. SHILLINGSBURG
Pegasus in Harness: *Victorian Publishing and W. M. Thackeray*